ELEVATE YOUR PERFORMANCE

ELEVATE YOUR PERFORMANCE

THE MOST INSPIRING WAY TO TAKE YOUR PERFORMANCE TO THE NEXT LEVEL

Foreword by Dr John Demartini
Human Behaviour Specialist, Educator & Teacher From 'The Secret'

Disclaimer

All the information, techniques, skills and concepts contained within this publication are of the nature of general comment only and are not in any way recommended as individual advice. The intent is to offer a variety of information to provide a wider range of choices now and in the future, recognising that we all have widely diverse circumstances and viewpoints.

Should any reader choose to make use of the information contained herein, this is their decision, and the contributors (and their companies), authors and publishers do not assume any responsibilities whatsoever under any condition or circumstances. It is recommended that the reader obtain their own independent advice.

First Edition 2022

Copyright © 2022 by Author Express

All rights reserved. No part of this publication may be reproduced, stored in a retrieval system, or transmitted in any form or by any means, electronic, mechanical, photocopying, recording or otherwise, without the prior written permission from the publisher.

A catalogue record for this book is available from the National Library of Australia

Creator: Harvey, Benjamin J., author.
Other Authors:
Davenport, Kerry | Dreger, Jase | Gibbons, Carole | Castellano, Irina | Harvey, Benjamin J | Hassan, Marty | Heald, Ivena | Mersinia, Dimitra | Pavlovsky, Trudi, Rettie, Andrew | Taumoepeau, Sēini F.

Title: Elevate your Performance / Benjamin J Harvey.

ISBN: 978-1-925471-62-5 (paperback)

Published by Author Express
www.AuthorExpress.com
publish@authorexpress.com

Dedication

*To fellow learners wanting to take
their performance to the next level.
This book is dedicated to you.*

Benjamin J Harvey and co-authors

Foreword by Dr John Demartini

In order to empower your life to the fullest and perform at your greatest most inspiring level, there are seven overlapping and interacting areas of life that are essential for you to take control of. These are spiritual, mental, vocational, financial, social, physical, and familial or relationships.

Any area of your life that you don't empower, someone else can overpower. The more areas you empower, the more you are in control of creating and crafting the life of your dreams. These are your seven greatest powers and they ensure that you are the master of your destiny more than a victim of your history.

These seven powers are most often undermined by their corresponding seven fears. These are: fear of receiving some spiritual authority's judgement; fear of not being smart or educated enough; fear of failure in business; fear of scarcity or loss of money; fear of rejection from close loved ones; fear of rejection from others in society; fear of not being vital or beautiful enough.

The number one reason why you may not be maximally performing in one or more of these areas and may be experiencing these fears, is that you are probably not living by priority or congruently and in accordance with your true highest values. It's the same reason why many of your New Year's resolutions have possibly not lasted. They were not fully aligned with what's truly most important and meaningful to you.

Everyone lives by a set of priorities or values, from most important to least important. Your highest values are those you're spontaneously inspired from within to fulfill. As you move down your list of priorities, you require outside motivation to start or sustain your more hesitant actions. When you set a goal that's aligned with your highest values, you will experience increased confidence, achievement and self-worth, and will therefore experience more lasting accomplishment and fulfillment.

If you are not performing at the level you would love and are not achieving your intended goals, it is at least partly because you are unknowingly trying to live according to your lower values or those of others. When you compare yourself to someone else's achievements, and try to imitate them you can lose focus and inspiration. When you compare yourself to others you admire and put them on pedestals, and put yourself in a pit, then you're trying to live by someone else's set of values.

In order to be the highest achieving you - it is essential and most empowering to spend your time doing what's truly highest on your daily list of priorities and delegate all other lower priorities to other qualified specialists. It is wiser to create or transform yourself into a lasting brand than by living vicariously through others and buying theirs. Building an inspiring and authentic life and being number one at being you is way more empowering than living with immediate gratifying consumerism through envy and attempting to be second at being others.

It is empowering to get clear about what's truly most important and meaningful to you and what you would truly love to go after, achieve and fulfill. Historically, most of the greatest performing achievers had a coach or mentor to guide them and help them not reinvent the wheel. Working with a quality coach or mentor that can help you ascertain your true highest values and assist you in achieving your goals can be wise and efficient. This can empower you and help you to more congruently structure your life, which can initiate ever greater action. When you do, you will be less likely to self-depreciate and procrastinate in your journey of performing and attaining your goals. Like for all great achievers when you live in accordance with your true highest values you will more effectively maximize your potential. So make sure you set goals and objectives that are truly deeply meaningful and most intrinsically inspiring to you.

One of the secrets to great achievement also revolves around the mastery of sustainable fair exchange and being of service. When you help enough people receive or fulfill what they would truly love, you help yourself receive what you would truly love and you truly make a greater difference. And if you're grateful for being able to serve, then you, too, will become fulfilled and *Elevate your Performance* in all seven areas of your life.

Dr John F. Demartini
Award winning Human Behaviour Specialist, International Best Selling author of 'The Values Factor'
www.DrDemartini.com

BONUS GIFT

The Elevate YOU
7 Day Transformation

Want to take the top 7 areas of your life to the next level?

There is ONE powerful 'Elevate Process' you can use immediately to improve Your Relationships, Health, Finances, Mindset and any other area of your life.

In this transformational 7 day online course, Benjamin J Harvey guides you through the "Elevate Process" and how you can improve your life from the inside-out.

Normally valued at $295
Get FREE and instant access here:

www.elevatebooks.com/you

Life Rewards Action. Get started today!

Contents

Purpose Driven Action — 1
Benjamin J Harvey

Performance Fundamentals — 23
Andrew Rettie

The Tipping Point — 47
Kerry Davenport

Personal Power — 73
Trudi Pavlovsky

Rapid Results — 95
Carole Gibbons

Unlocking High Performance — 117
Marty Hassan

Supported Parenting — 145
Irina Castellano

Futureproof — 169
Jase Dreger

Focus Your Flow — 199
Sēini F Taumoepeau

Achieving Holistic Performance — 221
Dimitra Mersinia

A Sporting Life — 247
Ivena Heald

"Giving yourself permission
to do what you love is the key to
elevating all areas of your life."

~ Benjamin J Harvey

Benjamin J Harvey

Purpose Driven Action

For over a decade, Benjamin J Harvey has studied the psychology of empowerment to help people find the answer to life's most intriguing questions.

Knowing that books like the Elevate series empowers individuals to bring their dreams into reality, Benjamin has assisted thousands of people across the globe to invest in themselves by showing how they can live their dream.

In 2009, he founded Authentic Education with business partner Cham Tang, to help empower people to live abundantly on purpose. As a result, Authentic Education went on to achieve something that has never been done before in the history of personal development. They received the BRW Fast Starters Award in 2013 and then backed it up in 2015 by being named in the BRW Fast 100 as the thirty-eighth fastest-growing company in Australia.

Having delivered well over 10,000 one-on-one coaching sessions, and training thousands of people across the globe, Ben now specializes in guiding people in how they can make a difference by achieving success doing what they love.

Ben has been featured on The Today Show in the Sydney Morning Herald and on ABC Radio.

Benjamin J Harvey

Purpose Driven Action

What's your top tip for someone to elevate their life?

It's simple! Do what you love. First and foremost, people need to listen to their heart and have the courage to follow that inner voice that already knows what they're here to do.

Every day I hear about people going to jobs they hate, suffering *Mondayitis* and just getting through hump day. Often it's because they don't know there's another way to live. Sometimes it's because they spent so much time and money obtaining a degree at university, they feel they need to continue in that role for the rest of their life. Other times there's pressure to follow in the tracks of their parents and be a doctor or lawyer, and along the way they forgot to follow their own authentic dreams.

I would choose doing what you love any day of the week over how much money you earn. There are many types of currency in life, and money is only one of them. I've had so many professionals coming through my programs who've had a successful career and now want to explore what they really truly want to do, rather than what they wanted to do when they started their career twenty years ago or more.

Most people spend a third of their time at work, so therefore one of your highest priorities in life should be having happiness and fulfilment in your career. The other two thirds are occupied with sleeping and recreation time.

In this chapter I will focus on elevating your life through your work and understanding what I call your Shadow Values.

Can money buy happiness?

When it comes to happiness, money doesn't mean a thing. There's the age-old saying, "Money can't buy happiness." Two-thirds (66%) of Australians value happiness ahead of pay, according to the 2018 research by Rise, the workplace meaning and happiness consultancy. However, due to a variety of pressures, the majority choose to stay in a job they don't like.

Also, in the study, 81% of Australians said finding meaning in their work would increase their overall happiness levels and 44% say that the pressure of not knowing what career they want is a major reason why they stay in their jobs. Given this finding, perhaps it's time to look for more inspiring ways to create fulfilling and meaningful careers.

We're all about encouraging people to live their love and earn a living while they do it, so no one has to feel unfulfilled in their job. We suggest that if you really can't stand the job you have, put the fears aside and start making some plans, because life rewards action.

How can someone get on track in their job or career?

We have identified five questions in a process called the Values TRACK that combine to create the ultimate career choice, one that you're guaranteed to be passionate about. The key to being truly fulfilled in your occupation is simple: just focus your space, energy, money and time on the areas that are in alignment with your Values *TRACK*.

Most people are so off track in life, that without changing their career it would be virtually impossible for them to ever find happiness. Knowing who you are is the first step to living a life of passion. Sadly, though, most schools only teach you how to get a secure job, not necessarily a satisfying one, so it's no wonder people don't know how to do what they love for a living.

Here are the five key questions we recommend you reflect on in order to uncover what you truly value and help you find the right career. You can also use the exact same method when looking at starting your own business doing what you love.

1. **Talk**

    What do you love to talk about?

    (For example: psychology, business or healing.)

2. **Research**

    What do you love to research?

    (For example: communication, spirituality or mediating.)

3. **Acquire**

    What skills do you love to acquire?

    (For example: presenting, coaching or sales.)

4. **Contemplate**

    What skills do you love to contemplate?

    (For example: solving the world's problems, traveling or quantum physics.)

5. **Know**

    What do you know a lot about?

    (For example: mindset, traveling or family.)

Once you know your top five answers, you can clearly see if the career you're currently in is on track with where your true value lies. If it isn't, then try something new.

My advice is simple: *get on track then have a crack*. Nothing is more important in life than doing what you love and sharing that with the world.

Why do you think people don't work for themselves doing what they're passionate about?

I think if we all gave ourselves permission to do what we love in life, the world would be a much different place. Most people worry too much about what others think, or they get caught up in their fears. Other times it's that they don't know how to make a difference and a fortune sharing what they know with others.

From working with thousands of people, I've come to realise there's something that's common to everyone, which is that they love to teach others what they know. It doesn't matter what the subject is, if it has to do with wellness, fitness, cooking, parenting, organising a home, starting a business, registering a trademark, building a business, writing a book, doing yoga, property investing or development, starting a restaurant, meditating or running a charity, there's always someone who wants to know what you know.

This is your message and a vehicle in which you can make a difference in the world. When you find your message, there are ways to monetise what you love to do by simply ordering and organising that knowledge. That's why it's called an *organisation*.

I often finish my presentations with the following sentence, which I think sums up the point I'm making here today: "Share your light, live your love and do whatever it takes to be your own best friend."

Why do most people continue working in a job despite being unhappy?

People often say they remain in their job because they need the money, but this is just an excuse they tell themselves, so they don't have to look at the real, underlying issue. Sadly, the majority of the time the real reason is because of low self-worth and a low belief in themselves.

The fact is that people who truly value and believe in themselves make sure they only spend their time doing what they're passionate about and that challenges them in some way. There's a quote from the book *Eat, Pray, Love* that I often think about when it comes to taking control of your life: "Balance is never letting anyone love you less than you love yourself."

I think it was Dr Phil who said that people end up treating you the way you teach them to treat you, through either your actions or non-actions. The real problem is not happiness in the workplace but the way you value yourself, love yourself and believe in yourself, but that's a whole other chapter!

How do we make the most of the job we hate, until we can do what we love?

What a fantastic question! It's easier than you would think.

Here's exactly what to do:

1. Imagine you had a magic wand that allowed you to have any career or business you desired. Wave the magic wand and write down whatever idea comes to you.

2. Close your eyes and imagine being in that career/business for a few minutes.

3. Open your eyes and write out at least a hundred answers to this question: *How does the job I'm currently in prepare me for the career/business I truly desire?*

The more answers you write down, the more you will start to see how your current job helps you progress to your future vision, and the more you see the value in what you're doing, the less you'll hate it.

What if I have to stay working in my job right now?

If you're willing to put in the effort, have the right attitude and work on your abilities daily, then you instantly become the most valuable asset of any organisation. When you think of any big brand, keep in mind it can't exist without its employees.

Once people wake up to the fact that they are the rarest commodity on planet earth, and that employment opportunities can be found anywhere, then they're able to take back their power.

All you need to do is jump on the website Seek to be reminded of just how common job vacancies are. There are literally thousands of them posted up each and every day. What's not common is YOU. You're one of a kind, and I can't get another one of you anywhere else in the world.

Once you realise this, you're able to make career choices from a place of high self-worth, and in doing so guarantee your happiness.

How can someone find their purpose in life?

There's so much pressure on people these days to find their passion and their purpose, and they're waiting for that *aha* moment or light bulb to go off to know for certain that they're on their path.

I'd like to take the pressure off firstly by saying your purpose can change at different times in your life, so just knowing you can have more than one purpose often is a relief. The next is that you need to actually go out and try new things.

One of the most common questions I'm asked is, "Do I really need absolute certainty in what my purpose is before I go out there and start taking the necessary actions to live the most fulfilling life possible?"

Here's my answer. I was recently running a seminar down in Melbourne, and I had the good fortune of speaking with a lady in the audience who mentioned she'd been sitting at home for well over three years virtually immobilized by how she didn't have unquestionable certainty and unstoppable determination, with the highest level of vision and mission possible, and as a result she wasn't able to move any way.

In fact she hadn't moved because she'd been convinced by the personal development industry that you must be crystal clear on your message, and I'm going to tell you that's an absolute load of rubbish.

You don't have to be certain about what you're going to do in life!

In fact, you can be as unclear as humanly possible yet still take necessary actions that will allow you to be fulfilled. When I poll audiences, quite often I find that most people have been out on some kind of date before.

Now, in a room of about five-hundred people I always tell them to raise their hand if they've ever experienced love at first sight and are still happily married or connected with that person today. Normally there will be about three or four people who raise their hand. That tells me that love at first sight is somewhat of an anomaly. It's kind of like finding a unicorn. It's rare. For the rest us mere mortals, the fact is that when we start dating people or going out on dates or getting into romantic relationships, we didn't wait till we were head-over-heels in love beforehand.

In fact, when you went out on that first date, you had no idea what that person was going to be like. You might have a bit of an understanding or seen a photo of them or maybe a friend referred you. The fact is, your first date *is not* really a date! It's nothing more than a deep psychological analysis of another human being, and you start to look at things like:

- how they're dressed
- how they talk
- if they make you laugh
- what sort of restaurant you're going to
- what sort of car they drive
- what sort of conversations you have

Based on that, you score them either plus or minus. For instance, if they look nicely dressed, you give them a plus. If you go outside, and there's a nice, fancy sports car in the driveway, you might give them a plus, but if they walk past that sports car and jump into a beaten-up 1960s Datsun Sedan, you give them a minus. After this little plus or minus game, at the end of your date you sit at home and work out if they had more pluses, even if it's just one more plus than minus, and decide to go on a second date.

This is the dating process at least for the first couple of weeks, and if you get more pluses each day, you continue to go on dates.

After a couple of weeks you start to feel a little bit emotional, a little bit connected. You feel something warm in your heart and realise you're starting to like this person you're dating.

As the weeks turn into months, pretty soon you'll start to realize you are, in fact, falling in love with this person you're dating, and of course you know what happens next. You'd sit them down, look them straight in the eyes and with absolute confidence say, "I love you!" They'd reply, "Excuse me, what did you just say? And you'd repeat, "I really love you!" They'd respond, "Sorry, you're going to have to speak up. I didn't hear what you said." Then you'd say, "All right, you got me. I LOVE YOU!"

I don't know if you've had an experience like that, but the fact is the first time you tell someone you love them, you're still not really sure if they're going to reciprocate and are a little bit cautious as to whether what you're feeling is real.

So is falling in love with someone the same process as finding your purpose in life?

Sitting at home wanting to be crystal clear and absolutely certain as to your purpose in life, is as insane as refusing to date anybody until you're certain you're in love with them, fully committed to spending the rest of your life with them.

Guess what? We've all been there before. Millions of people around the world are going through this process right now:

- They're sitting on a job they don't like.

- They're doing activities that aren't fulfilling.

- They're making just enough money to barely pay the bills, so they can go back to something they don't enjoy.

The reason they're doing it is because they've been sold this lie that until you're crystal clear with absolute certainty as to what your next step would be, you can't take it.

My advice is to start dating some new ideas.

If you like coaching, then:

- read a coaching book
- attend a coaching seminar
- call up a coach and talk to them
- read some psychology books to learn a little bit about mindset

Start dating in the evenings or weekends, and if you continue to like the date then my advice is to intensify the dating. Go from dating to *sleeping over*. This is where you might get a certification in coaching.

Then, who knows? Maybe after sleeping over at the coaching house, you'll *leave your toothbrush*, which means you may be start to go part-time at your day job.

Then you *place clothes in the wardrobe*, which is basically as committed as you're going to get. Next thing you know you've basically moved into the house, and that's pretty much when you quit your day job altogether, and you're fully and completely aligned to coaching.

Start dating! Don't think you have to be in love or certain.

People always say to me: *"Ben, what's it like knowing with absolutely certainty what you're going to dedicate your life to?"*

I have to tell you that I don't even know what that means. I have no idea.

All I know is that right now, talking to you is inspiring to me. Sharing this information with you to help you feel liberated and experience freedom in your life inspires me. I will tell you that if I wake up tomorrow and this doesn't inspire me anymore, I'm not going to do it anymore.

One of the greatest lessons I ever got from one of my spiritual teachers was this:

"Just because you manifest something, doesn't mean you have to use it."

So just because you create the most successful coaching practice you could, doesn't mean that if you started to love property you'd have to keep doing coaching.

Learn to live in a state of transformation, but certainly at least start dating some ideas.

If you like the stock market, then do some paper trades. If you like gardening, go and learn some gardening course at your local horticulture centre. If you like travelling, go and do a bit of travelling. Just see what it's like to go on a few dates. Before you know it, you'll start to fall in love, you've opened up your heart to your purpose, and then you'll be on your way!

Do you have an example of someone combining their purpose with their work?

We have students doing this all of the time. Our entire company was founded so that people can prosper from their passion. We run free events and trainings online worldwide, showing people exactly how to do it. You can find the programs, events and some of our client success stories on our website, www.authentic.com.au. There's one story I love that demonstrates our philosophy.

I remember watching The Oprah Winfrey Show many years ago. I think it was the one of the last shows she ever did. She was talking about some experiences in her life and recalled one moment when she went into a beauty salon, and this lady placed her hands on her face. Oprah said she felt a shudder of love go through her whole body. She'd never felt never anything like it in a beauty salon before.

At the end of it, she stopped and said. "That was the most magnificent thing that has ever happened. Can you tell me what the heck you were doing?" The woman said, "Oprah, *my whole life I've known my calling.*" And Oprah said, "Well, I talk a lot about calling. I'm a big fan of that." The woman said, "No, Oprah. My whole life I had to overcome the shame and the guilt and the judgement of others to follow my calling." And Oprah said "What's your calling?" She said, "Since I was a little kid, the only thing I've ever loved doing is extractions."

Now, if you don't know what extractions are, it's a fancy way of saying popping pimples. Everyone thought she was crazy. When she told her friends at school, they'd say it was disgusting and gross, and she put it away in a shadow. She was embarrassed by it. She kept going to her day job, until one day she thought, *Stop this! I don't care about other people's opinions. I'm going for it. I'm going to honour my calling!*

Oprah told the woman that it was the best thing she'd ever experienced, and did the woman want to come on her show and talk about it? Now, if you don't understand how the Oprah Winfrey Show worked, then you may not know going on there might bring a *small increase* to your results.

This woman now owns one of the most successful beauty salons in America. Millions and millions of dollars are going through that business now, because she dedicated her life to her calling. She gave up judgement, shame and guilt and replaced them with what she loved the most: popping pimples. That's it!

The moral of this story is to honour your calling. Forget shame, forget guilt, forget judgement...forget fear! Just do your thing, because there's one thing you should know about the world, and that is no matter what you do on planet earth, someone's not going to like you. It's just a simple fact in the whole game.

A great way to find your value is to think about if you have three hours to spare in the afternoon, what would you spend it on? You'd be doing what you love, right?

You can also attend one of our free events throughout Australia by signing up at our website, www.authentic.com.au, to see how you can live your love.

What are Shadow Values, and how do they help elevate your life?

Do you have behaviours that make you feel shameful, guilty, or even fearful? Does dwindling away hours scrolling through Facebook, or perhaps, sneaking a piece or three of chocolate late at night make you retreat in shame? These feelings have a name. They're called Shadow Values, and they're the driving force behind your behaviour, whether consciously or not.

Everything you ever do in life, every action you take, whether you realise or not, gives you fulfilment in one or many Shadow Values. I've spent over a thousand hours researching Shadow Values to determine what it is that unconsciously drives people's behaviour, and the findings are surprising.

By discovering a balance between your Shadow Values and Golden Values, which are the values you would happily tell the world about, you're truly able to bring mastery into your life. Everyone is seeking happiness on some level, but most don't know what it feels like once they arrive at that happy place.

Once people get over the shame and guilt they have around admitting the driving force behind their actions and behaviours, be that money, validation or even rebelliousness, people can take control of their lives. By taking ownership of your Shadow Values, you can leverage them to drive success, happiness and fulfilment in the most effective ways.

There are seven key Shadow Values I've listed below alphabetically, not by hierarchy. By understanding what your Shadow Values are, you can take ownership of them. Then once you own them, you own your life.

1. **Attention**

    Similar to uniqueness, status, feeling special, standing out, being different, prestige, recognition, achievement, adventure, creativity, variety, fun.

2. **Authority**

    Similar to giving orders, acting in an overbearing parent-like manner, being respected, having a sense of righteousness, having the power to do it all your way.

3. **Belonging**

    Similar to being accepted by, connected to or feeling part of a community, a friendship, a family.

4. **Control**

    Similar to being able to influence your circumstances, your territory, yourself and/or others, security, certainty, protection, safety, freedom.

5. **Rebelliousness**

    Similar to being naughty, knowing you're doing something wrong, breaking the rules, sticking it to the authority figure.

6. **Superiority**

    Similar to power, progress, expanding, success, ambition, achievement, confidence, morality, problem solving, being right, being better than yourself and/or others.

7. **Validation**

    Similar to being important, worthy and/or "good enough", deserving.

In addition to these, there are two other supplementary Shadow Values, which while not feeling orientated, were of significant importance:

1. **Money**

    Similar to being wealthy and/or having the power to do or have whatever you want, cash flow, equity, funds, cash.

2. **Sexuality**

    Similar to attraction, esteem, being able to express your sexual desires and/or preferences shamelessly, sexual intimacy, love, affection.

Once people are able to get over the shame and guilt around admitting what's at the core of their desire to do specific actions, they're able to rapidly take control of their lives. Until you're able to take ownership of your Shadow Values, they run your entire life. Once you take ownership, you can use them to drive your success, happiness and fulfilment in the most effective ways.

Using Shadow Values allows you to change any aspect of your life in a rapid and sustainable way. Everything you do in life gives you a feeling in return. Once you know exactly what feeling, or feelings, the action gives you, it can be replaced by another action that gives you a higher level fulfilment of the same feeling or feelings.

Here's an example:

Recently I met a lady in Perth who'd been smoking cigarettes for over forty years.

- She always wanted to be an author, however she'd never been able to start writing her book.

- She had a message inside of her heart she wanted to share, but for some reason she was never able to follow through with her action of writing a book.

I spent a few minutes doing some processes with her to help her move beyond her shame, guilt and self-judgement, so she was able to finally admit the core benefit she got from smoking cigarettes.

If you ask a smoker what they get out of smoking, more often than not they will say things like this:

- Nothing. I hate it.

- I'm addicted to it.

- I don't get anything from it.

People don't do anything in life unless there's some type of perceived payoff, so once they get honest with themselves, and are void of shame and guilt, they give a completely different answer.

This lady ended up admitting that every time she lit up a cigarette, she got a feeling of rebelliousness.

I then asked her how writing a book would give her an even stronger sense of rebelliousness, and she started giving me answers.

Once she'd given around ten to fifteen solid answers, she turned to me and said, "I've just quit smoking, and I need to go home now and write my book."

This happened in front of a live audience of around three-hundred people, and it was one of the fastest transformations they'd ever seen.

Even though it does seem miraculous when people witness it for the first time, this is a fairly standard result when Shadow Values are used correctly. Not only do people change rapidly, but they never crave the original behaviour again when the process is done correctly.

What happened with this lady, and the hundreds of other people who have achieved similar results, is a simple mathematical equation. This lady was receiving a certain level of fulfilment from smoking within her Shadow Value of rebelliousness. If we give it a score, it could be said she received a six out of ten for her rebelliousness fulfilment.

After answering the question regarding writing her book, she immediately realised she could give a nine out of ten for writing her book and therefore changed the behaviour right there on the spot. To her, smoking became a *lower-level fulfilment* in her Shadow Values system, and therefore she will never want to do it again.

In fact, anything less than writing her book each and every day would be robbing her of the feeling she so dearly loves to feel, that of being rebellious.

Human beings are bonding creatures with an inbuilt desire to bond with anything that gives them feelings they love. Once they bond to an action that gives them what they want at their core, they never again think about the actions they took previously to obtain a lower level of the same feeling.

At the end of the day the mind is set up as a *values fulfilling* mechanism, so once it knows it can get a higher level of fulfilment in a certain Shadow Value, it never craves the old behaviour again, because it's simply illogical for the mind to seek out a lower level of fulfilment in life.

The good news is that no one needs to feel any shame or guilt around their Shadow Values, because everyone has them. They're literally built into your DNA as part of your survival. They help you to evolve and advance your consciousness. If everyone has them, then there really is nothing to be ashamed of.

If you take a newborn baby and look at their behaviour, you can clearly see all Shadow Values being expressed on some level. For example, as they get all of the attention, they have total control of a room, it doesn't matter what you say, they'll do their own thing, and they require plenty of validation from their parents throughout the day. And all of this from someone who can't even walk or talk yet!

When you're able to find the perfect balance between your Shadow Values and your Golden Values, you're able to truly bring mastery into your life.

Every action you take has both Shadow and Golden Values, and this is why it's impossible to give without receiving in life.

For example, someone who teaches others may get these Shadow Values:

- **Attention**

The teacher feels this from being in front of a roomful of students looking at them for the entire class.

- **Superiority**

The teacher receives this from knowing they're delivering advanced content to the students most of them don't know.

- **Control**

The teacher gets this from being able to ensure the class runs smoothly by setting all of the rules and making sure everyone follows along with the lesson.

Looking at it from the student's side, you can also see the Golden Values:

- **Attention**

The students get the ability to learn in a live environment, because the teacher had the courage to stand up in front of a roomful of people and teach them lessons.

- **Superiority**

The students are able to further their education, because the content being presented is superior and thus advances their knowledge around this subject.

- **Control**

The students are able to learn effectively, because other students aren't running amuck, making noise and reducing the effectiveness of the learning environment.

You can listen to an audio program on Shadow Values by simply going to this link: www.authentic.com.au/shadow

So how do you master your Shadow Values when you're ashamed to admit what they are?

1. **Get Over It**

    Let's face it. We're all human, and we all have things we're embarrassed by. But everyone has them, they're inbuilt into the DNA, so the best way to move past that is to embrace them and understand how you can use them to better your life.

2. **Identify What They Are**

   Imagine you have the afternoon away from responsibility. What would you spend the afternoon doing? Whatever you choose is reflective of the greatest importance to your personal identity. For example, if you choose to visit with family, this may fulfil the shadow value of belonging. If you choose to study, this may fulfil the shadow value superiority. Just as Golden Values are arranged in a hierarchy of importance to you, so are your Shadow Values.

3. **Link Your Values With Your Goals**

   It's not Shadow Values themselves that make a difference, it's how you use them!

   If making money is important to you, and your Shadow Value is control, ask yourself how making more money can give you more control. Continuing from this example, do this exercise:

   a. Handwrite a list of three-hundred reasons why making money will give you even more control.

   b. Read it out loud before you go to sleep at night and again first thing in the morning for the next seven days while visualizing yourself doing whatever it is you do to make money.

   c. Walk around trying to emulate the feelings of being highly paid. Not *wanting* to be, but as if it's happening right now.

Once you've established how you can utilise your Shadow Value, you will no longer require motivation to take action, because you'll be inspired to do so by seeing what fulfilling your goal could achieve. In order to love yourself fully, you must first learn to love your shadow.

Then go about the business of living your love, and you will Elevate Your Performance.

To discover more about how Ben can help you *Elevate Your Performance*, simply visit www.elevatebooks.com/performance

Andrew Rettie
Performance Fundamentals

Andrew Rettie is a Fellow CPA with over forty years of professional, commercial, consulting and advisory experience in multinational-listed companies, SMEs and not-for-profits. He's held numerous senior management/executive roles, as well as operating his own business.

Andrew is passionate about what it takes for leaders to effectively reimagine their organisations, optimise performance and create a sustainable, vibrant culture.

Andrew works with entrepreneurial owners, new and established CEO's and senior leaders to build the necessary awareness, mindsets and capabilities to achieve their goals.

He enjoys the sport of rowing and exploring the world with his wife and daughters.

You can find more about Andrew Rettie at www.forayone.com

Andrew Rettie

Performance Fundamentals
'Our (Human) Nature'

What's the best way for people to take on life's challenges?

When it comes to *effectively* charting our course in life, solving problems or taking on challenges, I find it amazing that we don't fully understand our own (human) fundamentals!

The truth is, we don't know our full potential. This creates a conundrum when gauging our performance and comparing ourselves or competing with others. We have to accept that comparisons can't be conclusive, but they are helpful indicators of progress.

Fundamentally, once people become conscious of their own existence, they go on a journey of self-discovery and a search for meaning. We have to work out how we relate to everything around us, and most importantly, get to know ourselves! It's clear that realising our potential requires growth, which is part of our nature. Plus, we're hardwired to want more.

We also know that when people combine their efforts, they're able to amplify their achievements well beyond what can be accomplished as an individual. In fact, our species has relied on connection and cooperation to survive and thrive.

I find it helpful to put our individual reality and truth into perspective by recognising the three levels of reality and how they overlap and interact:

Level one: Nature is immutable

First, there's the Universe, our physical existence and the laws that make it so, even if we don't understand them all yet. This includes our own biology, mind, essence and energy.

Level two: Societal reality

This is the level people most experience as life. Social creation has developed and accumulated over human history and includes our systems for laws, rights, finance, privileges, social norms and culture. There's immense variety and variability in this 'construct' due to the constant forces of change, which human civilisations create.

Level three: Our personal reality

We 'construct' our own reality based on our unique journey and the environmental and influential factors around us, such as family, friends and communities. It's the third level, because the first two existed before we arrived, and we had no part in them. They would exist without us. This is the least reliable level because of the stories we tell ourselves.

When we don't pay attention to the forces or rules that govern the first and second levels of reality, we eventually experience *real* consequences. For example, if you ignore gravity (first level), it'll probably hurt you. And if you don't pay your taxes or drive on the wrong side of the road (second level), you're likely to pay a price.

The consequences of being out of touch or unaware at the third level are less obvious. You may be disillusioned or constantly bump into yourself and other forces around you. It could also be that you're unaware of the internal conflicts that block your own progress or being fulfilled in life. By ignoring your inner voice and bodily signs, you may become unhealthy, and even die. Your life might feel like it's being sabotaged by others, when in reality the person pulling the strings is you.

Andrew Rettie

It amazes me that we get busy with all the 'doing' without understanding our fundamental reality. We're guided and influenced by people close to us and what they deem to be true and valuable, even though they haven't worked it out for themselves. To be truly effective in taking on life's challenges, we need to start with ourselves.

What about your quest?

I trusted that if I worked hard and maintained a high level of curiosity, the answers to life's questions would appear, and my destiny would be revealed. Through quiet and deep reflection later in life, I realised that my own philosophy, my internal compass, had always been guiding me, consciously and unconsciously. Appreciating the power of my revelation, I captured its essence in a poster (shown below), which I'd like to share with you. It's on a wall in my office in a prominent spot and constantly reminds me of my quest for wisdom and expression.

Do you think people find the answers or create them?

I believe it's both. I stumbled across a quote that answered this for me. It's by John Schaar, an American scholar and political theorist:

The future is not some place we are going, but one we are creating.

The paths are not to be found, but made. And the activity of making them changes both the maker and the destination.

This was so powerful. I understood that, knowingly or unknowingly, we choose our path. The destination isn't fixed, and neither is the meaning. We create it.

How did this impact you?

I realised that I possessed all of the power and freedom required to make my life choices. I also accepted that along with this power came full personal accountability for the consequences and impact of my actions. This awareness didn't come gift-wrapped with guarantees. That's just not the way it works. I was also pleased to learn that neuroscience, physics and other bodies of knowledge, were coming together to support this realisation. You are in charge of your own fulfilment.

But most importantly, I understood that it was the same for everyone. It's what our humanity fundamentally shares, even though we try so hard to avoid or resist it.

This is common sense, really, but it wasn't so obvious in the actions of those around me, especially in business, and particularly during periods of difficulty. It's interesting that our attitudes around sport were different and more realistic.

I knew from experience that business and leadership were areas where I could make a valuable contribution.

What aspects of your life story set you up for this mission?

I'm grateful to say that my family and I have enjoyed a blessed life. We've been spared from serious traumas, disasters and the like. But we've had our share of challenges, surprises and financial problems to test us along the way. In hindsight, I've come to realise and appreciate all of these experiences have served us in one way or another.

I've lived in four countries, which exposed me to different cultures, standards of living, languages (however I resisted learning them), and a huge cross-section of people, attitudes and environments.

I was born in Peru in a mining town that was 12,000 feet above sea level. My parents weren't native to Peru or the altitude, which posed many lifestyle and health challenges because of the low levels of oxygen. By the time I was in my teens, I'd travelled to many beautiful locations around the world such as Tahiti, the Bahamas, Hawaii, Fiji and the Amazon jungle. I also experienced the pulse of amazing cities such as New York, L.A., Miami and London.

Attracting expats to work and live in difficult conditions brought numerous perks, as well as an appreciation of how important it is for companies to take care of families and staff. We had a close-knit international community of people and families who stayed connected long after leaving Peru. But due to a military coup d'état and the nationalisation of foreign-owned businesses, we had to leave. We moved to Sydney, but in the process, my parents lost much of their savings and the pension fund they'd been building up for over twenty-five years.

A few years later, we went to South Africa and then on to Botswana to continue working in the mining sector. We arrived soon after the Soweto riots, which certainly opened our eyes to the racial and inequality issues in the country, amongst other factors. In Botswana, we again were unwelcome, being the outsiders in times of change. Armed insurgencies and struggles were underway in several neighbouring countries, so life had its moments of vulnerability.

The catalyst to return to Australia was a change in the law requiring South African permanent residents to do national service. For me, it was simply out of the question, as I wasn't going to risk my life for an ideology I didn't believe in. I was the first in the family to return to Australia to pursue my studies and a career, and the rest of my family followed.

My original aspiration was to be a town planner, but a five-year degree and limited career options outside of local government convinced me to pursue another path. I chose accounting and economics as the basis for understanding business. I hoped it would open many doors and expose me to different experiences, which it did! I studied my degree at night and started working immediately in a small accounting firm.

My path changed course from professional accounting to commercial finance. I got an excellent education at IBM and met my wife there. Then I became finance director at the Walt Disney Company, where my responsibilities incorporated systems/technology and human resources. It was a highly demanding, yet stimulating experience. The entrepreneurial culture and drive were truly amazing to be a part of. This is also the wonderful time when my wife and I started our family.

The common denominator for working with great companies is being surrounded by high-quality individuals and professionals in a vibrant culture, which is something you take for granted while you're there. Invariably, when you work elsewhere, this quality really stands out.

My broader responsibilities at Disney led me to senior roles at other companies ranging from VP, to MD, to COO. These opportunities always entailed a growth focus and transformational journey to move the people and organisation from where it stood, to a higher level of performance.

Consulting gigs exposed me to many operational and strategic concerns, as well as leadership approaches and qualities, which is where my interest really ignited. For example, I saw how much more authentic the people and leadership were in the not-for-profit sector, where people were far more powerfully connected and aligned to the organisation's purpose. It also showed me that resourceful mindsets had more impact than resources.

Several projects exposed me to different forms of entrepreneurship. These are just a few examples:

- Attempting a consolidation play comprised of seventy or more IT service businesses of varying sizes. It required a lot of due diligence, which provided an in-depth understanding of the way people managed and led these businesses.

- Partnering with other people to create an early-stage venture capital fund that went to market just as the GFC hit. It's no surprise that we didn't manage to raise the minimum levels of capital within the required timeframe, but the insights I got from dealing with numerous inventors, inventions and investors, as well as R&D, certainly were valuable.

- Working with a business that was still acting like a start-up after fifteen years. They were cash-constrained, barely breaking even and highly dysfunctional. After a short period of transformational work, a strong valuation led to the business being sold to a UK public company, making the owner wealthy and setting the business on a new path.

People are the strength or weakness in any organisation. This was the pattern and story that kept repeating itself throughout all of my experiences and observations. I'm not dismissing other important factors by any means. I'm simply homing in on the most significant piece of the puzzle.

It comes down to the qualities of the entrepreneurs, senior executives and managers. I'm not talking about knowledge. There are a lot of knowledgeable people out there. Decisions, actions and behaviour aren't always based on knowledge or rational thinking. We often make emotional decisions that 'feel right' and then start looking for the 'facts' to support them. I'm referring to an acute lack of awareness, poor emotional intelligence and unrealistic mindsets, which are major obstacles to effective performance and teamwork.

I found that an important factor is the misconception of what it means to be a manager or leader. Jim Clemmer, from the Clemmer Group, describes the distinction between management and leadership perfectly.

- Management practices are about a *way of doing things*, which includes processes, systems, procedures and methodologies. (*Hint: people are not things, so people are not managed.*)

- Leadership is a *way of being*. This includes emotions, values, growth and culture, human attributes that go to the core of people and are the engines of behaviour.

In my experience, many managers, or those role titles that have direct reports, are often appointed or promoted for the wrong reasons, including

- having the best technical or functional skills in a team or group

- having deeper corporate knowledge and tenure.

Technical skills are vitally important, but the quality and workability of relationships in organisations are even more important for improving performance. Being good at the *ways of doing things* does not qualify you to lead people. For example, the best salesperson isn't the obvious pick to lead the sales team.

Peter Drucker describes leadership as the achievement of trust, and Simon Sinek says leadership isn't about being in charge, but taking care of those in your charge, which I wholeheartedly agree with. The leader's role is to support and clear the path for their people to succeed, because when they do, everyone succeeds. A rising tide lifts all boats. This is servant leadership, which is built on trust and care.

With respect to this leadership distinction, ask yourself if you're *being* the person who embodies the qualities needed to be effective in that role or merely *doing* the job and exhibiting expected behaviours. This question applies to every area of our lives. By way of example, refer to the image below, and ask yourself if you're aware of the difference between how you behave and who you're being in these relationships or situations. You should also consider how it affects yourself and others. It will definitely have an impact on how effective you are as a leader and the results you get.

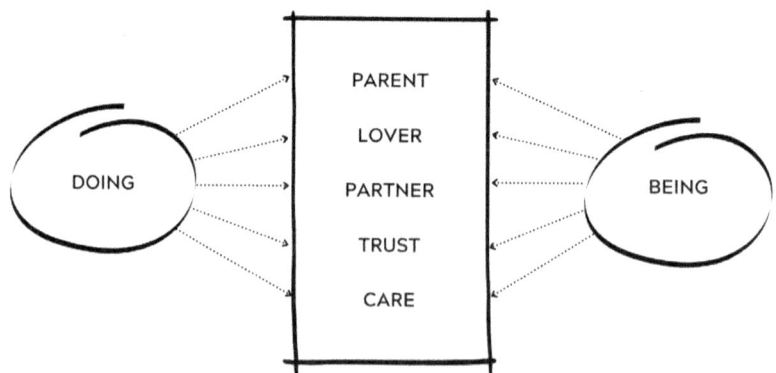

Improving individual and team performance begins here.

How did rowing influence you?

I learned rowing at school and loved the sport for many of the usual reasons. There were the physical elements, like being on the water, competition and achievement, and the social connection with people who shared similar values and mindsets. I continued rowing during my first two years at university but eventually stopped due to my expanding workload.

I returned to masters rowing a few years ago, after several decades away from it. Every time I saw ideal rowing conditions, I yearned to be on the water and in the zone again. I finally gave myself permission, space and time, and joined a local club. I should have realised sooner that early-morning rowing doesn't generally impede on your responsibilities, especially if you live close to the facilities!

So much had changed. There was a wider selection of boats and crew configurations. The technology and techniques had improved, as had the training approaches. I had to learn a lot of it over again, especially if competing was in the mix, which it was.

I keep seeing so many parallels between rowing and business, performance and leadership. It was impossible to ignore them. Here are but a few:

- **Purpose & Culture**

    Rowing boats and equipment are designed for speed, so there's an implicit assumption that everything you do is designed to make the boat go fast. You can take it easy, of course. To avoid the discomfort of building fitness, you can hold back on the effort needed, dabble a little through inconsistent training or pretend you're serious by only focusing on technique.

When compared to business, it raises the question of whether the purpose or ethos of an organisation exists and is clearly understood, and by whom. Equally important is whether the leadership and culture align authentically with it or not, and to what extent.

Many businesses start out as lifestyle decisions, under a misguided notion that self-sufficiency is freedom. But unless the entrepreneur actively grows or develops into an owner and leader, instead of just being an operator, they're unlikely to realise the anticipated success and freedom they desire. This is because the business is captive to the entrepreneur's or senior executive's level of personal development.

Large businesses tend to be preoccupied with scale and efficiency, human and systemic, for the sake of shareholders' returns, and everything that flows from it. This does little to inspire meaningful engagement, trust, well-being or growth in the very people and communities that make it happen.

Not-for-profits and community services are the most intentionally and transparently aligned organisations to their purpose, which is to deliver an authentic service built on care or value-adding to others. They can, however, experience the same mindset and leadership development issues of the other business types and sizes.

In rowing culture, your personal performance and goals are shared, and everyone knows the ground rules. There's power in embracing the truth, so protecting people from reality rarely serves them or others.

❖ **Mindset**

- Rowing is a sport that requires prolonged periods of concentration, precise execution and physical intensity, while remaining calm. It's an elusive balance of opposites. If you don't remain 'in state', your experience and performance soon deteriorate. In business, eliminating distraction pays big dividends in time, energy and engagement.

- In a rowing boat, everything you do has one of two effects: you either make the boat go faster, or you slow it down. This could mean you're working against yourself and your teammates, undoing your own hard work. Focusing on what matters and what's most effective, is essential to performing well. In business, shiny-object syndrome, 'present bias' or FOMO, work against everyone.

- It's easy and common to correlate size and strength with higher performance. They're important if applied effectively, but many times they're not. A common mindset I see in business is, 'If it isn't working, do the same thing, only harder and faster'.

You can spot a crew that's 'muscling' each stroke, working against the boat and exhausting themselves more quickly, thus depleting their energy in an unsustainable manner. And once they realise they're slipping, they try even harder to power their way back into contention.

In contrast, another crew that's maybe smaller and not as strong, calmly works with the boat with less effort, establishes flow and outperforms them.

- Rowing is influenced by environmental factors such as wind, tide and wash from other craft. We absolutely love ideal conditions, but they're not as frequent as we'd like. Every business is impacted by its environment, whether it's regulatory, technological, political, supply chain, resource availability or financial. We can learn to manage around the conditions and maximise our opportunities or suffer the environment. Where our focus goes, our energy flows.

- When you chunk it down, it's the things you can control that influence your performance. It's amazing to see how much time and energy goes into what we can't control, including the stories we tell ourselves to justify our performance.

- ❖ **Teamwork**

  ▸ Rowing is all about effective teamwork, just like business. Our world is complex, and a natural companion of complexity is fragility. No one person can know, master or do everything. It takes numerous people and trust. Regardless of the hero stories in our social culture, no one succeeds on their own.

  ▸ Teamwork is valid for a person rowing in a single scull or a larger crew. You need a coach to see what you can't, to direct your awareness regarding ineffective habits and to highlight changes in your performance under pressure. For teamwork to be effective, people rely on extremely efficient communication, partnership and trust. High-performing crews aren't captive to individual significance.

Many entrepreneurs and executives think and act alone, because they're reluctant to be vulnerable or need to be right. They often wind up exhausted, anxious, and more than likely, ineffective. Plenty of research suggests that CEOs are beset by stress, frustration, disappointment, irritation and exhaustion. While no CEO can escape these emotions completely, excellent ones know they will serve the company better by taking command of their well-being. But until they do, the rest of the organisation and results will definitely suffer.

Why are you focused on leadership?

Deepak Chopra is quoted as saying, "Leaders appear when awareness meets need. A person who knows what a group actually needs--the group can be a family, business, team, or political party--must be more aware than those in need... once the need is identified, the leader must take steps to fill the role that it demands".

The call for more and better leadership isn't new, but I believe there's a seismic shift underway in the demands and roles required of real leaders. Here are some of the ways I believe it's changing:

- ❖ **The convergence of forces**

    As citizens of the global community, we can see the speed and magnitude of the change that's around us. It's both amazing and confronting. There's universal agreement that the overall pace is increasing, and it will continue to do so.

    Advances in technology and access to information have been instrumental in creating this change. If you ask the majority of people, they'll say they've benefited and look forward to more advances but are now becoming more cautious about the impact.

    These shifts are affecting just about every paradigm or system at the same time. This includes the health and medical fields, our economic, political, educational and religious beliefs, as well as social justice, natural resources and the environment. These systems are beginning to unravel, break down and even collapse.

    There are also generational shifts in values occurring globally, and the populations of many advanced economies are in decline due to aging. Lately, the nature of work has changed, and this will have a long-lasting impact across societies and the economy.

    Mental health statistics all around the world highlight the toll it's taking on people. Tony Robbins explains it well when he says, "The quality of your life is in direct proportion to the amount of uncertainty you can deal with".

    How do we build capacity around uncertainty? Tips and tricks that lead to quick fixes are not the answer.

Change can occur quickly, but transformation takes time. It embodies change, so it serves you in an enduring manner. We must acknowledge that every person needs to have the skills and capacity to handle constant change, including ongoing transformational processes.

❖ **We live in an age of individualism and self-reliance**

Over the centuries, we became accustomed to being led in a paternalistic way by a king, governor, leader, teacher or religious figurehead. They disseminated information and gave direction on the basis of an ideology or system of principles and values. Today, society embraces individualism, which leaves many people isolated. Studies have shown that everyone is more connected through technology, but they're more alone than ever before. Connection, for most folks, happens at work.

❖ **Conversation around leadership**

The conversation around leadership can be about something exceptional, like changing the world or tackling major challenges, but is more commonly about position and power. We use the word like a title, which it is not.

The path forward is beckoning for alternatives that are mutually beneficial for all stakeholders, including the environment and society. Millennials, for example, are quite rightly rejecting old models and biases.

Why leadership in business?

I believe the answer is obvious. Business is society's common denominator and is most invested economically in maximising their people power on a sustainable basis. McKinsey & Co's research found that seventy percent of employees said their sense of purpose is defined by their work. Purpose is associated with belonging, so people *want* their work to align with their values and self-expression. It's a natural fit and mutually beneficial.

What will that mean for competition?

Traditional thinking has favoured financial measures above all else. However, the financial markets have informed us for quite a while that the value of most businesses isn't just based on its income or assets. According to Ocean Tomo LLC, ninety percent of the S&P 500 market value in 2020 was attributed to intangibles.

What is that intangible stuff? It's the human-centric elements of intellectual capital, reputation, trust, leadership, and culture, which is about results and consistent performance. This is why key people are retained in acquisitions.

In my view, competition is actually about hiring, engaging and retaining the best people. It's well-understood that the majority of employees leave their jobs and organisations because of the relationship they have with their direct manager or higher management. People leave people.

In-depth research from firms such as McKinsey & Co, Zenger Folkman and Deloitte Access Economics, find that CEOs who go beyond employee engagement and focus on cultural elements that drive performance, aka 'the soft stuff', achieve returns for their businesses over the longer term, up to three times more than companies that don't. That's a compelling insight.

These leaders understand that their companies *actually* compete on

- trust (far beyond just being well-intentioned)
- responsibility, authenticity and highly effective communication

- common purpose and principles
- delivering value to multiple stakeholders.

The real competition is for talent, which requires a shift in mindset and culture.

As an aside; when I'm asked to describe 'culture', I tend to offer the following:

1. What happens when the boss is away.

2. The way things are done around here.

I feel that 'the way things are done around here' is the better descriptor, because it neatly captures all of the elements, and it doesn't separate the boss from the situation. The executive micro-culture will inform and affect the broader culture, so the responsibility starts there. It also captures the impact of organisational and systemic elements.

High-performing cultures embrace the following principles:

- Adaptability and resourcefulness for multiple and shifting priorities.

- Agility, where speed and stability are combined, so people are constantly 'change ready'.

- A health focus, so people bring an abundance of energy and stamina, which is supported by a system that embraces work-life harmony. I use the word harmony, as I think it better reflects the reality than 'balance', which is generally perceived as an improbable objective. So, in essence, the principle needs to be reframed.

- Ecosystem models and principles found in nature that address all stakeholders and are being widely adopted in the software development industry, where it surfaced.

- A lifetime of learning, which is supported or provided by the business. It's investing in the business' future through its people.

What are other factors to consider in terms of competition?

❖ **Change or Transformation?**

The process of growing and creating a new culture in order to be more competitive and perform better, is a transformational process. Change can happen quickly but is unlikely to stick, unless it's integrated at a personal and organisational level.

Transformation takes dedication, commitment and consistent action, as well as time, space and investment, to ensure it's accomplished. It's the long game of creating the desired results, performance and value. There are no quick fixes, so it's not going to happen in a two-day workshop or retreat. Information by itself rarely changes anything. As Benjamin J Harvey emphasises, "Life rewards action".

❖ **Leadership Transformation**

Transformation work must always start with the entrepreneur, CEO or senior executives, as the case may be. To be effective leaders, *they must authentically lead from the outset*, so the people they influence can witness it, be inspired by it and follow it (seeds of the senior micro culture). The phrase 'If it's going to be, it's up to me', captures the essence of the process. It's not an initiative delegated to the HR department, so they can run a program or two with the staff.

Any journey of achievement always begins with a clear understanding of where you're really starting from. For an individual, it requires a truthful understanding of who you're *being* in all kinds of moments, and who you're aiming to be in the future. Closing that gap is the inner work you take on, usually with the support of a coach or mentor. Who you're being in every moment is not fixed. It can vary depending upon your relationship with that aspect, such as authenticity or compassion. You can be sure that people's vulnerability and integrity will be challenged, but their performance will improve.

You might find you're being hard on yourself, or maybe even beating yourself up, because of your own actions or lack thereof. This conflict or resistance carries over into how you interact with others and the relationships you have with them. In other words, how effective you are, which impacts results and performance.

You're probably aware that your internal dialogue is ten times that of your external one, so if you want to make an important change, where would you focus?

There's no question that your environment will trigger you, influencing your ability to make decisions and take action. Being aware of this and accepting that it happens and why, is a huge step forward in improving your relationship with it. Deliberately 'building muscle' around it, will improve your effectiveness.

What others see and judge you by, is your behaviour, traits and personality. Many of these may be fake or inauthentic, so merely focusing on changing your behaviour is unlikely to be a lasting and fulfilling solution. It won't be enough. Power and freedom will come from being real, authentic and vulnerable. These aspects of you already exist, so the route to change is just beneath the surface. Whatever you choose will come with a price.

This is the first step in your journey to authentic leadership, and by modelling these changes to others in your organisation, you will build the kind of enduring relationships that high-performing businesses are built on.

Expanding the process to your direct reports sets the scene for establishing or refining the principles and values that will underpin the culture of the organisation. Accountability is now shared. People have permission to call each other out when they don't live up to the agreed-upon principles and values or are not being who they promised they would be. This mutual accountability is done in a caring and constructive manner.

Only when your team is genuinely engaged in their own personal truth and transformation, will they be ready to model it to their people. Before you know it, there's a groundswell that lifts the business, and empowerment is unleashed, as they start leading from where they are.

- **Organisational Transformation**

    The entrepreneur owner, CEO or senior executives are responsible for the organisational design, where the technical or business systems enable the human systems to function and perform.

    The CEO is expected to sit on top of these systems and not in them. An objective vantage point is needed to ensure they're transformed in tandem with the leadership and culture. At the heart of this responsibility is care. Ultimately, it *all* affects the organisation's reputation, which is a core asset. A robust, professional support system is also crucial to ensure caring is balanced with high standards, consistent application and equity.

Andrew Rettie

How do you support business entrepreneurs and leaders in transforming their performance?

People are naturally at different stages and levels in their journey, and this includes their organisations. Furthermore, each person, group or organisation is unique in its needs and development, so I customise or align my services to match their needs.
There are common elements:

1. The first step in any journey is to know exactly where you're starting from. Being truthful and crystal clear about where you stand will make a huge difference to you and the journey you embark upon. This may include

    - a discovery process that embraces an understanding of what's actually going on and expanding awareness around it

    - an assessment to uncover high-value opportunities

    - an assessment of what existing activities or initiatives are in play, their status and what has and hasn't been making a difference

    - assessing readiness for change

    - assessing what behaviours and roles need to be adjusted.

2. Whether my client is an individual, group or team, each person completes a Being Profile, a unique ontological assessment created to assess qualities affecting performance, effectiveness and leadership. The Being Profile measures thirty-one distinct qualities across four separate categories that directly relate to an individual's personal performance in any area of their life and business. The framework cuts through the confusion of

behaviours, personalities, talents, traits and archetypes, to create clarity on what high performance in leadership and teams really looks like. It's an efficient building block to expand awareness and affect change from the inside-out.

3. Everyone already believes they're busy or full, and even overloaded, so creating space for expansion is important. This may require a conscious exercise in pruning, aligning or streamlining existing work. Without this step, no new initiative will be successful.

4. The creation or development process maps the starting position with the desired outcomes. In order to achieve and sustain them, the focus will be on people, which includes who they will need to be or become in the process, and the supporting micro and broader cultures. Jim Rohn captured this principle beautifully when he said, "If someone hands you a million dollars, best you become a millionaire, or you won't get to keep the money".

5. As part of our partnership, the approaches taken to empower and transform will align with the individual, group or team as required, including

   ▸ individual coaching or mentoring sessions

   ▸ group workshops for internal teams to uncover patterns that do or don't work, which includes building awareness and aligning individuals and systems to become a higher-performing culture

   ▸ facilitating groups of senior individuals from different businesses seeking a confidential, informed, supportive and sharing community of likeminded and growth-minded people who want to build their capabilities and awareness, as well as unpack key leadership topics.

6. Implementation plans, follow up and monitoring, form a part of the role we will play.

Sustained transformation requires focus, time, commitment and constant, repetitive action. There's no getting around that fact.

To build performance, you must empower and support your people to do what energises them. It's vital for sustaining momentum, and it's how performance comes to life. It will change the nature of the relationships inside and outside of the business, as you become a servant leader and witness performance growth.

To discover more about how Andrew can help you *Elevate Your Performance*, simply visit

www.elevatebooks.com/performance

Kerry Davenport

The Tipping Point

Kerry Davenport is a life coach, clinical hypnotherapist and keynote speaker, who's dedicated her life to helping others.

Due to her experience with Complex PTSD, she began looking at life's obstacles with curiosity and awareness, which led to discovering her true purpose.

As Kerry became more present, congruent and connected to the world, she was motivated to understand all of the modalities that helped her heal.

Fuelled by her past experiences, she successfully launched All Elements Coaching and Hypnotherapy, as well as the Tipping Point to Empowering Change program that educates, empowers and guides her clients to break the habit of reacting to life and begin responding to it.

Kerry Davenport
The Tipping Point

What is your biggest life lesson?

My biggest life lesson is that every obstacle we encounter and are tested by, is a chance to grow, learn and evolve. By refusing to look at past and future events, we delay our growth. I believe that being vulnerable and determined to face the pain of past events and emotions, takes courage, but in doing so, we're rewarded with the greatest gift of all… healing. This allows us to evolve further, to love more and to live a meaningful and connected life.

Something happens, we get a label or a diagnosis, and we unconsciously become that label. We then live in a bubble with our problems and close ourselves off to opportunities, change or transformation, because we believe there's no way out.

Fear, anger and grief aren't stopping people from achieving happiness and meaning in life. It's their resistance to these and other emotions. Suffering is caused by a reaction to external circumstances, not from the circumstances themselves.

To improve our lives, we can begin by replacing avoidance with awareness of what we're feeling. For instance, replace denial with acceptance and fear with acknowledgement. Tapping into your vulnerability can help release the resistance and suffering.

You can start by sitting still, doing some deep breathing and asking yourself out loud "What is it that I need to know right now?" Your unconscious will answer. You just need to be open and receptive to receiving the message.

Meditation is also a key way to connect to the soul. Many people say. "I can't meditate, because my mind wanders". This is just an excuse. When you were a baby learning to walk, you didn't turn to your parents after you'd fallen a few times and say, "Learning to walk is too hard. I can't do it, so I'm just going to crawl for the rest of my life". Why do we give up so easily as adults? Start with small sessions, be consistent and don't judge yourself. Judgement is just separation from self. The idea of meditation is to connect, focus and be present.

Showing gratitude for everything you've experienced in life is another way of raising your vibration to assist in healing and transforming your life. It does take courage and resolve, but the rewards are immense, powerful and freeing.

When we experience fear or anxiety, the body tenses up. This involuntary action reduces, and sometimes stops, the flow of vital fluids and energy around our body. The tension that's created can result in a large number dis-eases over time. I've worked with clients who've been diagnosed with illnesses such as fibromyalgia, high blood pressure, depression, diabetes, and so on.

First, I get them to take responsibility for where they are. Then we have a breakthrough session, an intensive one-day personal coaching session that's designed to help create a renewed sense of congruency, confidence and empowerment, together with the motivation to move their life in the direction they want it to go. Once it's completed, they're able to begin to release their major negative emotions, and all signs of illness disappear.

This is followed by Time Line Therapy® (TLT), which is a therapeutic process developed by Dr. Tad James, a master trainer of Neuro-Linguistic Programming (NLP). The client then releases negative emotions attached to past events such as anger, fear, sadness, hurt and guilt, they're able to extract the learnings, and the negative emotions dissolve. This willingness to be vulnerable gives my clients the opportunity to release the event once and for all, so they can create wholeness, peace and an empowering future.

Where do your passion and purpose come from?

Looking back over my life, I can see so many starting points, but I believe my passion and purpose became clear during the acceptance phase of my Post-Traumatic Stress Disorder (PTSD).

In 2017, I was diagnosed with Complex PTSD, severe depression and anxiety. I'd lost my short-term memory, and I was suffering from panic attacks, flashbacks and night terrors. The symptoms of PTSD had been intensifying since 2015. I kept thinking they would go away if I threw myself into my work, but they didn't.

At the time, I was a sergeant in the police force. I'd joined in 2000 after a five-year stint as a retained firefighter. Between 2015 and 2017, I fought hard against it, but I was becoming more withdrawn, anxious, depressed and totally frightened to admit anything may be wrong. However, I feared being ostracised or transferred, so I pushed through.

Finally, in June 2017, I succumbed to the nightmares, the sleeplessness, and worst of all, the total short-term memory loss. I remember feeling so soulless and lost, that I believed I'd failed at life. I refer to this period as going through the 'dark night of the soul'. It was a profound sensation of being swallowed up by a deep sense of meaninglessness that never ended. Nothing made sense anymore. There was no purpose to anything. I was fully disassociated from myself and my life.

It may have been a miracle, a *Sliding Doors* moment or universal intervention, but twice something stopped me from taking my own life. Eventually, I pulled my head, heart and soul out of the very dark and lonely void and began to slowly crawl forward in life again.

Over time, I finally acknowledged the dis-ease, accepted it, let go of my old identity and became curious about what PTSD was. That's when my life began to flow. It was a somewhat bumpy path, but nevertheless, it moved in a new and positive direction.

In May 2018, I walked into a Tony Robbins *Unleash the Power Within* weekend in a soulless state, and I walked out still with PTSD, but also renewed hope. My physiology and behaviour were changing, and I'd truly discovered my purpose in life, which was to use my experiences to help and guide others.

I began studying, learning and reading everything that intuitively connected and motivated me. My mind became a sponge. Whatever worked for me to heal, I went on to study, which included becoming a certified international life coach and gaining my Master Practitioners and Trainers in Time Line Therapy. I also completed my Diploma of Hypnotherapy and NLP, as well as many other certifications, after experiencing transformation as a client. Every course, book, blog and spiritual speaker helped me see clearer, heal and reinforce my knowing of why I was here on earth.

My own positive transformation became my driver to learn everything and more, so I could help those who were going through the same dark emotions. Today, I know my true purpose is to reconnect lost souls back to themselves and life. I'm extremely grateful for the opportunity to have experienced everything I have, as it fuels my passion and purpose to serve.

What are the symptoms of the dark night of the soul?

Here are some of the shared symptoms that can be found in both the dark night of the soul and depression:

- Everything seems to be breaking down.

- You feel confused, lost, meaningless, empty and lonely.

- You don't feel satisfied or experience joy in the things that normally make you happy.

- Life has no meaning or purpose, and you have an existential crisis.

I later realised that I had to go through what I did in order to bring about my own spiritual awakening. This process is also known as 'the death of the old self' and 'the birth of the true self'.

Eckhart Tolle describes the dark night of the soul stages in his teachings as follows:

- Stage 1: Deep despair

- Stage 2: Asking questions

- Stage 3: Seeking answers

- Stage 4: The Path is shown to you

- Stage 5: Finding your life purpose

- Stage 6: Meeting your soul tribe

- Stage 7: Spiritual awakening

I remember only hearing about these stages when I was at stage two. In a strange way, it gave me hope. If you, or anyone you know, is experiencing symptoms of depression, Eckhart's writings and teachings may bring some hope and peace.

What was the one thing that when you got it, everything else seemed to fall into place?

In some ways, everything started to fall into place when I began to accept what was happening, instead of worrying or being fearful of all the 'what-ifs'.

At the time I was living with Complex PTSD, in total overwhelm, not knowing if I would be able to keep my home due to being unable to return to policing. I was really struggling with what I referred to as 'the mind monkeys'. I didn't know where I would live, if I would recover or what had caused my severe anxiety.

I remember this one simple but profound aha moment. One day, I finally dragged myself out of the house to clean the old pool in my backyard. I was rhythmically vacuuming up and down, up and down, and just staring into the tranquil, hypnotic blue water. Then, out of nowhere, this vivid voice came to me. It said, "Without your health, you have nothing".

I remember looking at my home, and then back at the water, while thinking about how materialistic things were irrelevant compared to my health. It was a real turning point in my recovery. I started to invest in my own therapy, education, and training, and the more I invested, the better I got. I stopped focusing on the what-ifs and instead concentrated on what I had: my goals and my recovery. Deep inside, I was connected to a knowing that everything was happening for a reason. I just had to stay present, trust and allow. I learned to embrace the journey from that point forward.

What you perceive, you receive. As my clients begin to see and feel this, it becomes their tipping point of empowering change, and the journey takes them from where they are to where they truly want to be.

The greatest investment you will make in life is in yourself.

If you were speaking to your younger self, what advice would you give?

The greatest advice I could give is, 'You are always loved, whole and complete'.

What do you think stops people from having a healthy self-esteem as an adult?

It's important that we treat our internal child and adult self with a sense of balance and love. Growing up, many people were told to suppress their childlike behaviour in subtle ways that included these kinds of statements:

- "Grow up".
- "Be a man".
- "Stop being a baby".
- "Stop being so sensitive".

These well-intentioned comments can cause the inner child to disconnect and go on to create self-worth issues as an adult.

Society has taught us to reject our childish side, so we can grow into an adult. But in doing so, we're rejecting, abandoning and banishing our inner child.

More and more evidence proves that most root causes of trauma spring from those early couple of months before, during and after birth. From when we're born to the age of seven, we're in what's known as the imprint period. We're a sponge, absorbing everything we hear, see, taste, smell and feel. Our parents and caregivers do their best to teach us based on what they were taught and experienced, but quite often their emotions and limiting beliefs are unintentionally passed on to us.

What role does early childhood trauma have on our adult life?

When I was seven, I was on the veranda of our home with my mum and nan. My mother had just told me I was adopted, and I was trying to get my head around everyone not being who I'd believed they were. I had questions going through my little brain like *Why was I given away? What did I do wrong? Why did they not love me?* I couldn't understand, because I was too young, so I bolted to the backyard, got on my little push bike and pedalled away.

Working through all of the emotions of being adopted, including abandonment, lack of self-worth and belonging, would come much later in life. The running away from the pain would also remain a habit I would unconsciously implement, until I was much, much older.

Even though we probably can't remember what we saw, heard or felt as a young child, our body does, and our behaviour as an adult can leave clues.

The inner child is always part of us. It can help us heal and let go of past traumas that are no longer serving us, and continue to haunt and hurt us as adults.

The adult part of us is rational and responsible. That's our conscious mind. The inner child is our emotional response. It's an innocent, joyful and creative energy. When you're lonely, depressed, angry or even unloved, it means the adult you is feeling disconnected. These painful emotions can lead to habits and addictions, all of which can be destructive in relationships and affect our own mental health. When we reject our inner child, we're denying a part of ourselves the opportunity to heal and be whole and loved.

Today, I'm extremely grateful for the family that adopted me and the mother who gave birth to me. Without any of them, I wouldn't be here right now. It was the ultimate sacrifice to not only give me up, but also invite me in.

The purpose of your life challenges is to heal the inner child. Emotions are like children that need to be acknowledged and loved. Just as you are not your physical body, you're also not your emotions. Approach them with compassion, curiosity and understanding, rather than resistance and fear.

After working with me, my clients come to understand that these past events and traumas, once acknowledged and released, have no further impact on them. The memory that remains no longer triggers them or causes pain.

Your life challenges are valuable teachers. When we can go within, while having no judgement or shame, we learn to release the charge of these negative emotions.

Inner child therapy sessions assist clients in releasing past trauma. They're encouraged to look at their childhood with honesty, because it's difficult to heal from any emotional or mental issue, unless it's approached with empathy. As an adult, it's easy for us to judge, blame and condemn ourselves, but it's much harder to do this to our childlike selves. Acknowledging the inner child as a separate entity helps us disconnect from our own judgements, which allows true healing.

This simple yet effective form of therapy empowers clients and sets them free from pain. It allows them to create love, achieve connection and evolve.

Have you had any aha moments that changed everything for you?

As you think, so you become. Since releasing my past negative blocks and reconnecting to myself, one of my biggest aha moments, and there have been many, was grasping the mind-body-soul connection. I truly believe the relation between energy, emotions and the physical body, is so important to understand. Candace Pert, in *Molecules of Emotion*, writes:

> ...We can no longer think of the emotions as having less validity than the physical, material substance, but instead must see them as cellular signals that are involved in the process of translating information into physical reality, literally transforming mind into matter.

Emotion is energy in motion, and it needs to be able to flow freely. If we ignore past traumas and suppress our emotions, they will crystalise in our cells and chakras. This creates blockages, which creates dis-ease. When you feel an emotion come up, focus into your body and where you're feeling it most. Then follow that feeling back to where it began. Just by acknowledging and getting curious, we can begin to release the blockage and start the healing process. In turning our focus inwards and being vulnerable, we can break up the crystals of emotions and move freely again.

When our body experiences an injury, illness, or dis-ease, it's sending a message that we're out of balance. This is nature's way of creating symmetry. Unfortunately, the first reaction is often to think, *Why me?*, *Why now?*, or *I don't have time for this*. Once people are presented with dis-ease, most tend to jump over to the effect side of the fence and believe they're a victim of life. But the truth is that it's been created because we've missed the more subtle clues that needed to be addressed.

By being present, intuitively listening and allowing ourselves to be vulnerable, we can release energy blocks before they're created. When we don't take the time to be present, tune in and learn, we force our mental and physical self through the dis-ease, and all of the medications and medical actions that come along with it. The trapped energy in the body will still be there, and if not released, will just manifest in another way, sometimes even stronger.

In 2013, I experienced an extended period of intimidation from a work supervisor. After approximately six months, I awoke one morning with a bulging disc in the C4/C5 in my neck. Within one day, I was unable to lie down at all. I was taking the strongest painkillers possible, and still the pain was overwhelming and debilitating. The next four weeks were a blur of agony, medications, tests, x-rays and MRIs. After being told I would need surgery, I stopped taking most of the painkillers and started focusing my attention inside my body to figure out what the pain was trying to tell me. I started acupuncture and gave myself Reiki, which is a Japanese technique that promotes healing. It can treat the whole person, including the body, emotions, mind and spirit.

At the time of the injury, I was in the middle of a four-month training plan for a big ocean paddling race in Hawaii. We were due to leave in seven weeks, and the first thing everyone said when they saw me was, "You definitely won't be doing that". But, inside of me, I had this knowing that I wouldn't need surgery, and I'd be participating in the race.

The neck communicates both physically and emotionally. It's the bridge between our thoughts and feelings, as well as our minds and hearts. Problems in the neck can indicate rejection or a lack of energy moving through into the body. The neck contains our voice box, and is intricately connected to our self-expression.

A stiff neck can represent a limiting belief that you're unable to express, or a feeling you're holding back, and the emotions are too strong to express. It could also be that you feel something or someone is emotionally strangling you. While studying for my hypnotherapy diploma in 2017, I realised that all of these emotions and feelings were present in me during that time.

We went on to complete the 52km race at a steady, methodical pace that guaranteed us a strong chance of finishing. My neck returned to normal without any surgery, and upon my return from Hawaii, I was given the opportunity to move to a new location and work with a supportive, guiding supervisor.

The whole experience was a massive aha moment to me and opened my curiosity even more to the link between energy, the mind, the body and suppressed emotions.

How do you help people deal with their past traumas?

For my one-on-one sessions, I try to make my clients comfortable by offering either a more clinical setting or walking and stand-up paddle-boarding coaching sessions. Outdoor activity stimulates emotion and rhythm, which sparks energy in motion. The more we move, the more we can connect with our emotions to assist with healing.

In my eight-week Tipping Point Program, you will work on understanding your current mindset and learn how to make empowering changes.

Each week you will build a greater connection and understanding of your true self and develop a meaningful mindset practice. You'll become more present and aware of your actions and decisions, which allows you have more control.

Following is a breakdown of the program:

Week 1: Discover your core strength and internal drive, and develop a meaningful mindset practice.

Week 2: Master your awareness and the power of being present and accountable.

Week 3: Dissolve obstacles, limiting beliefs and undesirable behaviours.

Week 4: Learn how to activate your intuition, so you can move closer to your goals.

Week 5: Uncover your sabotaging behaviours, and create empowering forward momentum.

Week 6: Discover your internal compass to help enhance all areas of your life.

Week 7: Master self-love, communication and your relationship with others.

Week 8: Release trapped emotions, create meaningful goals and discover how to achieve your freedom.

The Tipping Point Program helps you create rapid and long-lasting change that will improve all areas of your life. It dissolves obstacles like limiting beliefs, self-doubt, self-sabotage and emotional baggage that are stopping you from living your full potential.

You'll discover your purpose and direction, especially if you're at a life intersection or just know you were born for something greater.

This ten-week, eight-session program is conducted both face to face and via Zoom. It's structured to provide answers, guidance and empowering techniques to help you move forward with inspiration and passion.

"When you know better, you do better" is one of my favourite quotes from Maya Angelou. It can be applied continuously in every area of our lives.

How did you become interested in hypnotherapy?

In 2009, a friend referred me to a hypnotherapist after I returned from a work deployment. I had constant sugar cravings for ice cream, alcohol, biscuits and chocolate, constantly binge-eating anything with a high sugar content.

During the six sessions, the hypnotherapist worked through a number of old negative emotions I thought at the time were totally unrelated matters, but would come to understand later were connected to several root causes of my cravings.

Following my mother's passing in 2009, I hadn't allowed myself time to grieve and instead threw myself into my work and sport. Over time, I created a belief that I'd dealt with everything, and I was fine. This limiting belief couldn't have been further from the truth. As time went on, my behaviour and addictions were leaving some noticeable clues, but because I was in denial, I was oblivious to them.

Even though I loved my mother, we had a very distant relationship. All of these suppressed negative emotions were being ignored, and I was unconsciously utilising quick fixes to get a short-term high from sugar and alcohol.

As we went through the hypnotherapy sessions, I discovered that I had deep underlying feelings of abandonment. After I was told I was adopted, I really hadn't processed any of it.
Hypnotherapy allowed me to reconnect with the inner child I'd run away from to avoid the pain. It was a coping mechanism that helped me create the independence to survive when I was young, but as an adult, I understood it was time to let go of those 'stories'.

Today, I'm so grateful for that experience, especially when I see similar behaviours and addictions in clients. Children who are adopted, fostered or even separated from their parents when they're extremely young, can harbour feelings of abandonment, guilt, shame and lack of belonging, all of which are buried in their unconscious. These emotions are quite often unrecognisable, or the events happened so long ago, they're not linked together. Our behaviours, addictions and personalities, along with illnesses and diseases, are all clues that something deeper may need addressing.

This experience was a turning point in my life, where I became open and receptive to learning and growing spiritually. It fuelled my curiosity and desire to learn more about the mind, body and spirit connection. I went on to study several forms of energy healing, including becoming a Reiki master, while I was still working as a police officer.

Today, I'm a fully qualified clinical hypnotherapist and trainer. I inform all of my clients that any form of addiction, from food and alcohol, to gambling, gaming, and shopping, or even an over-committed life, can be a form of escapism. It's an indication that our inner self is clogged up with repressed emotional energy, which creates contradictory, distorted feelings and false beliefs. It's like a volcano, bubbling away under the surface. It doesn't matter if it's five or fifty-five years later. It will eventually manifest into some form of adverse behaviour, illness, disease or injury. And if it's not acknowledged and released, emotions such as helplessness, loneliness, desperation, anxiety, depression, anger, guilt and suicidal thoughts, can arise.

Brené Brown is a research professor at the University of Houston who's spent the past two decades studying courage, vulnerability, shame and empathy. In June 2010, during her TEDx Houston talk on the power of vulnerability, she shared the following:

> *The problem is— and I learned this from the research—that you cannot selectively numb emotion. You can't say, "Here's the bad stuff. Here's vulnerability...here's grief...here's shame...here's fear... here's disappointment. I don't want to feel these. I'm going to have a couple of beers and a banana nut muffin". ...*
>
> *You can't numb those hard feelings without numbing...our emotions. You cannot selectively numb. So when we numb those, we numb joy, we numb gratitude, we numb happiness. And then we are miserable, and we are looking for purpose and meaning, and then we feel vulnerable... And it becomes this dangerous cycle.*

What are the most important lessons you've learned?

My biggest learning is that when the student is ready, the teacher shall appear. They may arrive in the form of a person, book, podcast, movie or course, and even a program. If we're open and receptive to learn, evolve and heal, the universe will drop the breadcrumbs of opportunity for us to follow. How we act or react to this information will have an impact on us.

During my Practitioner of NLP training course, there were so many profound learnings and life-changing moments. For instance, I discovered the importance of eye patterns, including how we construct and recall with just the movement of our eyes (see the chart below).

EYE PATTERN CHART
AS YOU LOOK AT THE PERSON

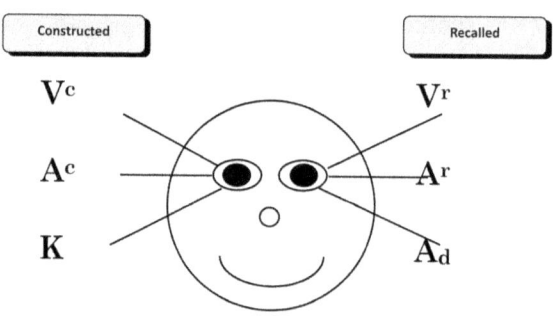

V^c = Visual Constructed
V^r = Visual Remembered
A^c = Auditory Constructed
A^r = Auditory Remembered
K = Kinesthetic (Feelings)
A_d = Auditory Digital (Self-talk)

Up until the age of fifty, I'd always struggled with spelling and grammar, having had dyslexia since I was a child. I didn't read my first book until I was twenty-five, and I constantly spelled words the wrong way or the way they sounded. Sure, I got by, I failed and resat a lot of exams, and spent double the time other students did completing assignments. Other times my fear overtook me, and I just totally avoided working in areas or studying qualifications.

Underlying all of that was a large amount of self-doubt and the belief that every time I had to sit a test, write a report or do anything associated with grammar and spelling, it would be a major struggle.

Limiting beliefs block you. By allowing myself to be fully open and receptive, I let go and became filled with new knowledge, confidence and excitement.

I went on to do my Masters and Trainers of NLP, so I could help others. During a five-hour written exam, I utilised several of the techniques we'd been taught during the course, from spelling strategies to putting myself into a learner's state. I scored one-hundred percent in that closed-book exam. Today, I teach and share all of these techniques, and many more, during my one-on-one consults and my Tipping Point Program.

What do you think people's biggest problems in life are?

That's a great question. I feel one of the biggest problems people have is identifying as a diagnosis or label. These are some examples:

- "I have depression, and my life is over".
- "I'm a victim of assault, and I'll never trust anyone ever again".
- "Because my dad left, I never had a role model, so I didn't know any better".
- "I have ADHD and can't learn".
- "Because she hurt me, I can't enjoy life anymore".
- "If I didn't get retrenched, my life wouldn't have been ruined".
- "My mum was an alcoholic, and that's why I'm like this".

We're all constantly living between cause and effect, with cause being empowering and effect being disempowering. When we live on the effect side of life, we often blame others and are full of reasons why we don't create results. We live as the victim in our own pity party. It's like we're in a box buried under our problems and can't see past them. It's not until we step out of the box by taking responsibility and being accountable, that we're able to take control and create empowering change.

The constant belief that you've been victimised by something or someone, reduces your energy and vibration. The lower your energy goes, the more susceptible you are to illness. Think of your vibration as a rechargeable battery. The happier and more joyful you are, the more charged and full of life you are, and the stronger your vibration will be. Victim vibration drains the life out of you. By moving to the cause side of life, your battery can start charging again, and your vibration and energy will rise. Living on the effect side of life is like getting on a bus without knowing its route. The bus will take you places, but it's not necessarily where you want to go.

If you're constantly relying on receiving sympathy from those around you, you're sabotaging your recovery and making it harder to leave victimhood. The more sympathy you get, the more you justify your feelings, and the longer you stay there.

Many support groups surround you with well-meaning encouragement. However, some keep you in the victim state as they continue to unintentionally treat you like one. You bond with others who also believe themselves to be victims. People love sharing their story with other victims. This is natural behaviour, but it creates a disempowering state. The pity party is lonely and unfulfilling, and has been experienced by everyone at some time. It's how long we choose to stay there that matters, as it can lead to numerous illnesses, including depression.

For example, let's say your parents separated when you were ten, and you didn't get to see your father again. You're now forty-three, bankrupt, been married twice, don't get to see your kids and you're an alcoholic. You blame all of these circumstances on not having a father figure in your life. This is called 'mastering victimhood'. We're all victims at different times in our lives, but how we act or react to life from that point forward will have the biggest impact on our future, our behaviour and our well-being.

By choosing to be in cause, you become the driver of the bus and are therefore the creator of your own life. Working with an experienced life coach or therapist will empower you to take responsibility for your life and make the necessary changes.

I present regularly on different life challenges to groups and businesses. Cause and Effect always generates the biggest aha moments.

Please see the diagram below for examples of Cause and Effect.

Cause	Effect
Responsibility	Reasons
Results	Excuses
Solutions	Blame/Limitations
Empowerment	Disempowerment
Control: Driver of the Bus	Passenger on the Bus
	▸ I'm a victim, because...
	▸ I deserve pity, because...
	▸ I'm lacking, because...

Why do you think so many people are overwhelmed and unhappy with their life?

From my experience, both personally and as a life coach, I believe there are several reasons why so many people feel unhappy. It nearly always starts with a disconnect from their true self, coupled with a perception of how things 'should' be, followed by an adverse reaction to life, instead of accepting and embracing it.

The result is that we suffer from the stories we tell ourselves. These are some examples:

- "I will never be happy".
- "I'm not good enough".
- "I'm not smart enough".
- "I'm a victim of ………".
- "I have to do what I'm told".
- "I need to do this for my… (mother, father, spouse, friend)".
- "My father was an alcoholic, which is why I'm this way".

These are just limiting beliefs and stories that keep us trapped.

Reacting to events in life with anger, fear, guilt or frustration, will also contribute to your suffering, both in the short and long term. When you're feeling anger, you can't experience joy or happiness. So for every minute, hour or day you spend in a negative emotion, you're unable to enjoy what's happening around you. If you hold onto your negative emotions, over time you will eventually manifest illness or disease. Like attracts like, so if you're constantly angry, you will continue to attract anger into your life.

For example, if someone cuts you off in traffic, you get angry and frustrated, even yelling and screaming at them. The tension caused by the anger is now affecting your body. You become tense, your heart rate rises, your jaw clenches, and your shoulders and neck become stiff, all over an incident that lasted a few seconds.

But the suffering gets worse, because you then go to the trouble of communicating the story repeatedly, taking your body back into all of the toxic feelings and emotions, and you carry the reactions and physical effects throughout your day. To add insult to injury, the anger begins to show up in your relationships and interactions, as well as other areas of your life, because you chose to focus on this one event.

There's a saying that goes, 'Holding onto resentment is like drinking poison and hoping the other person will die'. Our bodies aren't designed to remain in negative emotions. For instance, anger causes tension, which in turn creates blockages and stops the natural flow of energy throughout the body. When the energy doesn't flow, dis-ease can be created. It's similar to a river that's blocked, and the water becomes stagnant and murky, causing the life within and surrounding it to die. Our bodies are the same. Trapped emotions stop our flow of energy, until eventually our system clogs up, and we die.

The mind, body and soul constantly try to let us know something's not right. But if we're not in tune and present, we just connect with our ego and push through it. They say that when there's a problem, at first it's like being tickled by a feather. If you ignore it, then you're hit by a rock, which is then followed by a brick. And if you still don't listen to your intuition and take action, you will get hit by a Mack truck.

The universe will get the message through to you one way or another. I've had several clients who kept repeatedly pushing themselves to work longer hours and didn't eat or sleep well, which resulted in them being constantly tired, stressed and moody. Slowly, their health started to deteriorate, relationships failed and they had to take more and more medications. But still they pushed on, believing that one day soon, they'd take time off work. They just needed to make more money first. But tomorrow never came, and they suffered several major illnesses that forced them to listen to their body and assess their lives. We don't need to be hit by a Mack truck to take action. We just need to notice the signs when they're a feather.

The more we push something away or fight against it, the more it will come back. Resistance creates persistence. If you beat a challenge in one area of your life without learning the lessons from it, you will discover it manifesting in another. Peace, joy and healing are not created by beating anything, but by embracing everything.

I encourage my clients to first acknowledge the obstacle, and then accept it and get curious about what their body is trying to tell them. I ask these questions to provoke them into understanding what's going on:

- What could be the message behind what's happening?
- What thoughts did you have prior to this obstacle appearing?
- What do you need to know right now?

What was your tipping point?

I remember waking up one morning after several months of living in the darkest, lifeless hole imaginable. My own dark night of the soul. I was sitting on the edge of my bed, when out of nowhere I asked myself out loud, "What the eff... is PTSD anyway?".

This was a turning point for me, I finally acknowledged the obstacle instead of living in denial. That question, and my acknowledgement, led to my own acceptance and the beginning of a life of curiosity, healing and learning. Instead of closing myself off to the world, and more importantly, the universe, I began to open up, tune in and become connected again to my soul.

How can someone learn to let go and enjoy their life?

There's a quote by Carl Jung that I love. He says, "The gold is in the dark. And one does not become enlightened by imagining figures of light but by making the darkness conscious".

Life doesn't happen to you, it happens for you. Sure, you will still have your ups and downs. We are, after all, nothing more than pure vibration and energy. It has to ebb and flow, or we die. Life also has to ebb and flow. We must know the night to appreciate the day. My favourite saying is "This too shall pass". Sometimes the ebb is a new obstacle to learn from or an old challenge that we haven't yet embraced, accepted and learned from. Either way, it, too, shall pass if we don't ignore or fight it.

When you begin to accept, embrace and learn during your life journey, initially it may feel like you're going uphill. There's so much to take in, accept and change, especially if you've been in avoidance and sabotage for a long time. I compare this to a plane having to reach cruising altitude before it can change direction. You're working your way back to the tipping or pivot point. You want to get back to being balanced, connected and one with your mind, body and soul.

What's the biggest tip you could give these people?

Suffering ends when you know and accept who you are. The more disconnected you become from your true self, the more suffering you will experience in your life. You are the carrier of your emotions, but you are not your emotions. You're a spiritual being having a human experience.

It's all about choice. Life doesn't happen to you; it happens for you.

The heart isn't awakened by anger, even if it's for a just cause. Behind every feeling of anger is fear, and that means you don't trust the flow of life and are in a state of vulnerability. Your greatest challenges are never about what other people do or say, but how you respond and react to them. To rise above your negative emotions, you need to acknowledge, accept, and appreciate why you're experiencing them. Having perceptions of how things *should* be or what people *should* do, will bring you frustration, disappointment and tension. Remember that expectations are the death of joy. Becoming trusting and forgiving of yourself will set you free as you mirror this externally.

 To discover more about how Kerry can help you *Elevate Your Performance*, simply visit

www.elevatebooks.com/performance

Trudi Pavlovsky

Personal Power

Trudi Pavlovsky is a coach, facilitator and speaker with over ten years of experience. Her work across the globe has introduced people to the power of physical, mental, emotional and metaphysical practices to create lasting change.

Trudi is well-known for creating unique experiential 'games' programmes that encourage teenagers and adults alike to rethink how they view the world and themselves.

In 2021, Yahoo Finance scored her in the top one percent of performance coaches in Australia out of a pool of over 2,500 coaches.

Trudi has taught in schools and adult education programmes, mentored new coaches, is a Reiki Master and has previously been an NLP Master Trainer for an RTO.

Trudi Pavlovsky

Personal Power

If you were speaking to your younger self, what advice would you give?

I would tell myself, "Stay true to who you are, and really listen to that inner voice".

I can look back at my past now and know I refused to listen, because I didn't realise what intuition or an inner guidance system actually was, and I certainly wasn't able to trust that inner voice. I probably could have saved myself a lot of pain and heartache if I'd just trusted myself more.

How would you like to be remembered?

I think I'd like to be remembered as being kind and authentic, which I know is a word that gets thrown around a lot. But to me it means showing up as who you truly are, not bowing to the dictates of society and expectations of others, and being brave enough to speak your truth, even if it's not popular.

What is the one message you wish to share with the world?

You need to give yourself permission to ask for help.

I love hearing people say, "Hey, there's this thing inside of me, but I don't know how to share it or how to shine my light" and asking for help and support. We're told we should be able to figure everything out and do it on our own. But knowing that what you need is already inside of you, and letting people help you shine that forward is the key to truly living a full life. You lose time holding back and slowly figuring it out. So take advantage of the time you have now, and get the support you need to become all you can be.

Are there particular people we should ask for help?

I think you should ask people who are taking action. It's easy to ask those around you, but if they haven't lived and experienced it, they're not necessarily going to be able to give you the right support.

This is one of the reasons I have two coaches and other mentors. I put my hand up, and it fast-tracks me up the ladder after years of biting my tongue. You don't ask your cousin's best friend for financial advice when they're broke and barely able to pay the rent. You talk to a financial adviser, an accountant. You ask people who are living and doing the thing that you see for yourself.

It's important to ask the right people, and that's where coaching comes in. Working with a well-qualified coach who's attained the level of success you desire, is critical for your success.

So it might be that your whole family has always worked a job, but you want to start your own business and become an entrepreneur. They're not the right people to ask, because quite often they will hold you back, thinking they're doing it out of love and care for you. They don't have the experience or understanding, and it's scary for them, so they will try and warn you about potential failure. They don't see the advantages, because they haven't done it.

For example, it took my mum nearly eight years to stop asking me when I'd go back to having a real job, because her model of security was budgeting her money based on her weekly income, rather than managing the ups and downs that come with working for yourself. Because of her limited experience, she couldn't see the unlimited potential for earning.

Trudi Pavlovsky

What decisions have made a difference in your life?

Well, a less-than-positive one was listening to the wrong people when I was in my twenties. I became a little sheep, following my friends and partying. I didn't save any money, which meant I couldn't buy a house or plan for my future. It was a terrible situation.

But on the positive side, I finally decided to learn about coaching, so I could take charge of my own mental health. After a series of bad decisions, I was depressed and self-destructing, and nobody was able to help me. They would give me Band-Aid solutions like, "There's a medication that will make you feel better," or, "Stop being friends with those people".

The best decision I ever made for myself was to say, "All right, I'm going to figure it out. I'm going to do some research and look for answers. I'm not going to accept these over-simplified solutions. I want to look for something deeper and long lasting". And that's when I actually discovered personal development.

When I was in my late twenties, I'd seen an ad about life coaching in a newspaper that I pinned on my notice board. Six years later, I decided it was time to find out what life coaching was, because I was miserable and not progressing anywhere. I knew deep inside me, I had so much potential and was here for a purpose, but nobody around me was lifting me up.

That's when I realised I had to stop waiting for a knight in shining armour and be my own rescuer. I eventually went and did a certificate four in life coaching, and it was the best decision I ever made.

What do you think is your life purpose?

I'm a teacher and facilitator. Sharing my own life experiences, and the wisdom I learned from the abuses I faced in my childhood and early twenties, gives my life meaning. I went through all of that pain, but I didn't succumb to it and learned to stop playing the victim. I've been able to find meaning from it, and I can support other people in fast tracking their healing through relating my own experiences.

I definitely feel that my purpose is to help people live their ultimate happiest and fulfilled life.

How old were you when you realised that you were the one who had to take control?

*Trigger warning- suicide topics

I had three suicide attempts when I was in my twenties.

Roughly, these happened when I was twenty, when I was about twenty-five and when I was twenty-eight. After the last one, I woke up in my car down by the beach. I'd cut my arms open, and there was blood everywhere. I'd vomited on myself, because I'd attempted to take pills and just about anything I could get my hands on to end it.

But it didn't end. And there I was, watching people walk past my car. No one was paying any attention to me, and I realised I couldn't keep living this cycle. I didn't know at that stage how to break it, but as they say, third time's the charm. I sat there wondering, *Why am I still here? There has to be more to life than escaping pain through parties and drugs.* Even at a young age, and through all my battles and traumas, I knew I was here for a reason.

During my school years, people would say to me, "You're so smart. You're so talented. You're so skilled". But even though I'd won an award for musical theatre at seventeen, I didn't feel it. And when they told me they couldn't wait to see where I wound up, I felt like such a fraud.

So there I sat, covered in blood and vomit, with friends and family trying to call me, because they knew something was wrong, and I thought, *I* can't live like this anymore. The only person I'm hurting is myself. Those people who hurt me are in the past. They don't care. The men that raped and abused me, the bullies at school, the absent father. All of them... they don't care.

And that was a real turning point to me. It made me realise I was the one common denominator in my life. So I asked myself, *Why am I letting them hurt me still? I'm better than that. I'm smarter than that.*

So out of absolutely hitting rock bottom again, like a phoenix rising from the ashes, I knew I had a choice. I could either stay in that space or choose a different path.

That was the moment. It was so powerful. I don't think I can really convey in words what it was like.

It made me appreciate how much stronger I was than I'd given myself credit for.

It wasn't an easy process.

There was a six-month drug detox, and I had a lot of relationships to repair. My first mission was going out and finding a full-time job. I'd only been working sort of casual and part time, while trying to keep it together and partying a lot.

I was shifting my focus from the past to looking forward again, one day at a time. Yeah. I feel like I was coaching myself even before I really knew what coaching was.

What do you think people's biggest problems in life are?

Living up to what they think they should be instead of what they truly desire, and not understanding how past experiences are constantly forming their beliefs around who they are now. But if you don't know this is happening, how do you sort of moderate that? You don't.

You need to understand how you were raised, the possibly faulty beliefs and values you live by and if you're honouring them, because the values and beliefs formed in childhood are created from a childish understanding of the world.

Certain events that happened when you were young could be driving you. For instance, if you're seven years old and something bad happens, you might believe the world is out to get you. And as an adult, if you haven't addressed that belief, you'll unconsciously continue to maintain it. How do you live in that space where you suffer and struggle? I see people living in needless distress and martyrdom, because they don't understand how the past impacts their ability to move forward.

What's the best way to help these people?

Well, look, obviously to me, the first thing to do is get a well-trained coach. They're going to be able to take your beliefs, remove the energetic charges in the neural pathways of your brain and clear them, which allows you to gain wisdom, so you can move forward.

If you notice a pattern of behaviour is still showing up in your life, or if you're feeling a certain way that doesn't feel good, explore it and pull it apart in your own brain. Ask yourself why you feel this way, where it comes from, what you can do to release it and what it could mean for your life going forward. I think awareness really is that first step. Become conscious of traumatic situations that keep occurring in your life and if you're feeling a certain way that's not serving you or helping you grow, because this is a sign it needs to be addressed, worked on and healed.

What's the biggest tip you could give these people?

Instead of giving away our personal power, we can give ourselves full permission to make decisions and accept the resulting choices that come from them, which allows us to feel good and live our best lives. It's the first step in removing the shackles of society and setting yourself free of the past that no longer serves your present and future aspirations.

Because to me, that's what life is. You make choices about what you're going to do and how you're going to act. Make decisions that work for you. Give yourself permission to put yourself first.

Something my mentor, Ben Harvey, always says is, "I'm allowed". I've always had a Post-It Note affixed to my door with that message, and I look at it before I leave the house. It helps me remember that I'm allowed to feel good. I'm allowed to show up powerfully, fully expressed in the world. I'm allowed to speak my truth. I'm allowed to have nice things. It's a constant reminder that I don't have to ask permission from anyone to live my most fulfilled and happiest life.

What do you think inspires people?

I believe many people look externally for motivation. But I think when you're truly honouring yourself and your values, you're internally inspired.

When people stop seeking permission, allow the internal inspiration to show up for them and honour their values and beliefs by doing what they want to do, they don't need anything external to validate them at all.

You can get excited and inspired by what other people are doing, but it has to be a match to who you are. When you're seeking inspiration, look at the things you love, at what excited you when you were a child, whether it was painting, running or playing a musical instrument, and go back to those things, because the past has clues.

I've done this in my own life with singing lessons and dance classes, and it brings me so much joy. My inner child is so happy too!

Do you have an approach to your performance?

I realised that if I wanted to perform at my best, I needed a total mind-body-emotional approach. When I added the metaphysical, it became complete. For example, if I have a presentation to give, I allow myself the space to rehearse, even though I've had people say, "You're really good at speaking. You don't need to practise." But when I listened to them and winged it, I wound up feeling like I'd let myself down, and my performance wasn't at the level I knew I was able to achieve.

Now I not only practise, but I also make sure I look after myself in other ways, especially when it comes to my mental and emotional health.

I do a lot of visualisation to support the metaphysical. When I'm taking action from the performance space, I want to make sure I'm at cause and fully owning what I want to create, knowing my energy is in the right space. I'm not just talking about my physical energy, but emotionally as well, as this impacts the vibration I'm sending out into the universe.

Side note: I also need to get enough sleep.

Because I work with the mind and body, as well as the emotional and metaphysical aspects of life, my mindset has to be right, and I have to feel good physically in my body. I still work on my mental health every day, I'm very aware of how I'm feeling in my own mind and thoughts, and what I'm vibrationally, energetically sending out to the world. I also work with my clients in regard to these four elements to get them to a good place.

I developed a fixed mindset as a child, and understanding this allows me to manage my performance. I find joy in the whole journey towards my goals, which allows me to operate at a higher performance level, when previously if I didn't 'nail it' on the first go, my imposter voice would show up, and I'd often quit.

How do you work on your mental health every day?

I've spent a good thirty-plus years really hating myself and telling myself I wasn't worthy. I know those pathways are heavily myelinated in my brain, which makes it easy to think less than loving thoughts about myself. If there are times I haven't been honouring myself or getting enough sleep, and something isn't working in my life, I can automatically go back to telling myself, "You're so stupid. You're such an idiot" and really flatten myself. But I catch it and ask if it's true for me now, and the answer is always, "No, it's not. Something didn't work, but it's not the end of the world". So, I'm aware of my thoughts, because they become things. The energy behind the way you speak to yourself impacts your results.

How can someone find their life purpose?

Many, many years ago, when I first got into personal development, I did a course with a gentleman named Christopher Howard. The process he took us through was going back to when we were young, because like I said earlier, the past leaves clues. Those things we say to ourselves when we're kids have a lot of energy, right?

You need to ask yourself what you liked to do when you were young and if it's something you could study, research and potentially turn into a new career. Or maybe you stay in your job, but you find other ways to get that same sense of fulfillment and purpose. When I was younger, I wanted to be a teacher, and I feel that I teach now, but in a different way from what the title meant to me then. I also wanted to be a psychiatrist. When my teacher said she didn't think I knew what they did, I told her I wanted to help people feel better in their heads. Again, I do that now, but from a different perspective than my original childlike interpretation.

When I was young, I also wanted to be a performer. My first business was all experiential games where we dressed up as different archetypal characters to teach teenagers life lessons.

My suggestion is to look at what used to light you up when you were young. To me, it's the best starting point, because so many people realise their purpose after going through this process.

What are your tips for getting through a difficult time in life?

Acknowledge how you feel, and be okay with it. If you need to cry, cry. Let the feelings out. Don't trap the emotion in your body, and stop pretending that you're okay if you're not. Let it out. Speak it, share it, get support. I think one of the toughest things for people to cope with is being isolated and feeling they can't reach out and express themselves.

Through my own experience, I realised I had to be okay with not being okay, and knowing that it does get better. This is where getting support, and then learning how to take care of yourself to continue feeling better, are critical.

I just get so frustrated that this kind of stuff isn't being taught within the education system.

I'm hopeful this is changing. It's been six years since I worked with teenagers in the education system, but even back then I kept thinking we could go further with teaching personal development. I'm always pleased to see others have taken up the charge in that area.

What mindset do you believe is needed to create a great life?

You definitely need to be willing to fail. I only use this word, because people understand it. But I think it's more about being willing to keep going and not remain attached to a particular outcome. This is sort of a metaphysical thing as well. People know about the law of attraction, but I'd like to educate them about the law of repulsion. When you get attached to things having to be a certain way, that's when, from an energetic perspective, you start repelling what you want.

You need to be open to knowing what you want, but also not persistently stuck on the idea of how you get there. Give yourself flexibility. It makes life so much easier. Just keep reminding yourself, 'I know I want (this thing), and I'm going to take these steps to get there, but I'm also open to other possibilities'. Be receptive to opportunity and potential, because if you're blinkered into only one way, you miss all of the ways you can get you what you want at a potentially faster rate.

You're so positive as well. Is that an important part of mindset?

Remaining positive is important, but not at the expense of pretending everything's okay. I've encountered people who were so focused on being positive, that anything negative got pushed down, buried, ignored. But these experiences also need to be acknowledged, because they're not going away. And if you push stuff down for too long, you get the explosion. It's like holding a beach ball under water. You can only hold it under for so long before it pops up to the surface.

I'm a positive person now, but not to the extent that I block out anything that's less than positive or might be considered negative.

I don't watch the news, for example, but I'm still aware of what's going on in the world. I just don't immerse myself in an hour of negativity every night. I'll get my snippets, and I have sources that keep me up to date with what's going on. I'm constantly aware of what I'm digesting, what I'm reading and who's around me, which helps me stay in a more positive framework, but not at the expense of ignoring everything else.

Something Ben Harvey teaches that I'm absolutely aligned with, is that forgiveness is *not* the final stage of healing. It's a wonderful stage of the process but it doesn't stop there.

As with anything having to do with your mindset, whether it's positive or negative, that final step is getting the wisdom from whatever the experience is. Being open to learning is something a lot of people are missing. That healing/mindset/getting better sort of framework space.

How do you start your day?

I've taught myself to be a morning person, because I realised sleeping in until ten a.m. was, for me, symbolic of being depressed. As a result, most mornings I wake up anywhere between six and seven a.m., and I generally start my day with visualising how I want it to go.

How did you teach yourself to be a morning person?

It's a little bit embarrassing. I was extremely motivated because of a man.

But he shined a light on my sleeping in when he asked me what it really meant and wondered what was really going on. That's when I realised I had to step up and address this. I'd had a pretty challenging year both personally and professionally, so I had to assess what the benefits were to waking up earlier versus what I had to lose, and I realised I had more to gain. I just started setting the alarm earlier and booking early client appointments. Then I had to get up and be ready for my clients, because at that point, I needed external motivation to get me moving.

A month later, I was getting up and going for a run at 6:30 in the morning. It made me remember the beauty of a sunrise and how fresh the air was, not to mention the peace and quiet. I wound up dropping ten kilos and began intermittent fasting. It was the next level of transformation for me.

My morning visualisation is probably the most powerful thing I do. It's like a memory you haven't experienced yet. I get to see my whole day laid out as if I've already completed my tasks, which makes it easier to take action.

How did your dancing fit into your life?

When I was like seven or eight years old, *Young Talent Time* was on television, and I wanted to be on the show. I would pretend I was a contestant while singing into a hairbrush microphone for hours in the lounge room to mum's records and the radio.

However, my mother was a single mum who worked really hard to put a roof over our heads and feed her kids and stuff, so there wasn't any money for dance or singing lessons.

It was a good thing I had a big imagination. I grew up in a little country town, and when I was sixteen, we had a debutante ball. I made my to-do list and started learning dances. The teacher would tell me I was a natural, but unfortunately I was late to the party when it came to competitive dancing, because most kids start by the age of ten.

I ended up leaving school at the end of year 11, so I could get a job to pay for my dancing and dresses. Two years later, I wound up moving to Melbourne because my intimate partner was moving there, and started dancing at a new school. I didn't get to professional level, because I ran out of money, and it was challenging finding a dance partner who was at the level I was at the time.

I only seemed to find ones who wanted to date me. And of the last two dance partners I had try outs with, one ended up stalking me, while the other yelled abuse at me, because I told him I didn't want to date him and just wanted to dance.

It was messy, and threatening, so I stopped. But that's when I discovered nightclubs, which satisfied my desire to dance, as it was always about the music and the movement.

I went back to taking dancing lessons in 2019, but I had to stop due to injury. Then I was going to try again in 2020, but that's when Covid hit. I started back for a few lessons later the next year, but then I injured myself again.

The goal is to get back to dancing again. And even if I just do my exams and get that fitness going, I'll consider myself a success, because it's something I've always loved.

This goes back to living your most purpose-filled, happiest life. I'm never going to be a dance teacher. I'm never going to become a professional, but I love it, so why deny myself?
This is why at forty-seven, I've also started singing lessons. You have to give yourself permission to pursue what you love, even if you aren't that great to begin with.

How does visualisation help?

There are three levels of the brain which all need to be activated to move you forward. This is where visualisation comes into play.

If your hindbrain deems you're safe going to dance class or taking art lessons, then there's no reason to be suspicious of it, and you'll have a level of certainty about being able to do it. This brings you yet one step closer to easily achieving the goal of finishing the task.

Your midbrain works in pictures, so it needs to see you doing these activities. Be it dancing, singing, applying for your dream job, or attaining your ultimate partner. If the midbrain sees it happening, you've activated level two!

Once these two parts of the brain are on board, the neocortex, or the forebrain, can then take action.

Visualisation stops the sabotage and self-doubt. It's part of the process of allowing you to live your life, set goals and create and achieve them. Visualisation is huge for me. It should be for everyone.

I spend a lot of time in my head, feeling and imagining what I want, like it's a memory and not a goal. You should give it go!

Did you start with visualisation as part of your process with personal development?

We did visualisations when I first started learning about coaching and doing personal development events. But when I did Benjamin Harvey's Authentic Education coaching program, I finally understood why we do it, the way it works with your physical body and how it triggers your brain to allow or disallow sabotage.

It's really only been within the last six or seven years that I've understood how to consciously use this to my advantage.

Do you have a visualisation board, or is it all in your head?

I do a lot of it in my head. I've had vision boards before and actually ran a vision boarding course, but I tend to just do my day to day in my head. I have some pictures up on my wall, but that's it.

What do you believe holds most people back from achieving the lifestyle they desire?

Fear of failure and fear of success. Knowing what I do about how the brain works, our cellular setpoint and how our cells respond and react,

Elevate Your Performance

I can say that what holds people back is that they're not being honest with themselves about what they really want. They don't understand how they can get their mind and body, including their emotional and metaphysical states, to work in their favour.

It wasn't until the end of 2018 that I embraced metaphysics. It was a huge, huge transformation on top of everything I've done.

I believe that people don't make powerful choices. Women especially don't decide for themselves in their own favour. I won't get on the feminist / patriarchal bandwagon here. That's for another day. In my own lived experiences, and the ones based on most women I've worked with, females are brought up learning to martyr themselves for others, while men are taught that they have to be stoic and strong. As a society, we think this is all there is. As I talked about earlier, if people gave themselves permission to do what they wanted and loved, and got the support that would help them break through what's holding them back, the world could transform so quickly.

What stops someone from achieving that success?

If you're not achieving the success you desire, chances are you're living someone else's life, or are following someone else's rules.

I spent a few years listening to a former coach tell me what I should be doing in my business, even though I kept saying it wasn't what I really wanted. In the end, I followed her rules. But even though I learned and grew from the experience, I'll never get that time back.

You need to ask yourself if you're living your best life, or the one other people are saying you should.

Again, this goes all the way back to your childhood dreams. Have you denied them, or are you living your best life on *your* terms?

What are your favourite ways to relax and enjoy life?

I love walking. I love getting out of the house and seeing what's out and about. Lying on a couch with a cat on my lap just sipping a cup of tea, is also time well spent. I love to dance. I'm setting up a training program with my physiotherapist and have committed to dancing fifteen minutes a day, four days a week. I model and love planning really creative photo shoots.

Any way of being that allows me to express myself is so important to me. They light me up, and that brings me joy.

How can people be happier in life?

I think it's important that people are honest with themselves about what they want. A big thing I had to do for myself, and now do for my clients, is removing any shame and judgment around doing what you love. It's about letting go of the guilt of wanting things that maybe those around you don't have. As a society, I feel we're weighted down with judgment, guilt and shame, and the feeling that you have to suffer to be worthy.

You don't have to suffer. There's no need for it.

I did a massive healing process with my coach at the end of 2018 to let go of this God trauma I'd had from childhood. When I was able to release a whole heap of that and heal my wound with God and the masculine, it showed me that we do live in a beautiful, abundant world with enough for everybody. When we give ourselves permission to say, 'This is what I want for *my* life', it can't help but transform you.

What was the one thing that when you got it, everything else seemed to fall into place?

I think it goes back to waking up in my car and realising that nobody was going to rescue me. I had my loving mum and stepdad and beautiful friends, but I told myself that I had to stop waiting to be saved.

Ultimately, you need to understand that anything you want or don't want in your life is your decision to make.

Do you recommend any spiritual practices to keep someone at their peak?

Metaphysics, also known as universal or spiritual law. The final piece for me was healing the God wound and my trauma with the masculine. It brought together the rest of my personal development work. Everyone knows the law of attraction, but they're less familiar with the law of repulsion, the law of vibration, the law of cause and effect and the law of correspondence. I would suggest doing a little bit of research around these subjects, as well as cellular energy and your cellular set point.

Everything is energy sending out some sort of vibration, and like attracts like. So if you're sitting there in a space of misery, don't be surprised if you're surrounded by miserable people. If you're focused on looking for the joy, looking for the lessons, looking for the positive, you'll start attracting people who think the same way.

When you're raising your energy, vibration and setpoint, what happens quite often is that people who aren't growing with you, naturally fall away. This was something I personally had to come to terms with and accept. But I needed to put myself first, because sitting in a hole with these people and being miserable, wasn't going to serve me in living a purposeful life. I'm okay if people don't want to take the journey with me, but I love being surrounded by those who do.

Is there a book you would recommend for people to learn about metaphysics or cellular energy?

Google is your friend. But if you're new to personal development, I'll tell you what's on my personal bookshelf to help get you started.

Trudi Pavlovsky

The first book I ever read before I knew about coaching, was *Feel the Fear...and Do It Anyway* by Dr. Susan Jeffers. It really opened my eyes to what I could become, and that I no longer had to be a victim. There's *Big Leap* by Gay Hendricks and *The Five Love Languages*, which is a little bit of a tangent from performance. But understanding how you and others receive love, improves your ability to connect with them better, which does elevate your performance. It was quite good for me to understand as well, because by nature, and maybe by nurture a little bit, I'm not the most physically affectionate person. I was always meeting people who needed lots of hugs, and I couldn't understand why. It really helped me relate to them.

How do you look back on the most difficult time of your life as someone who's now come so far and done so much work on yourself?

I have much empathy for that girl who just didn't know there was something else, and I admire her for her courage to make the decision she did at the time. I look back and realise it could have gone either way. I could have picked up the razor and just kept going. I could have gone back to *partyland* and pushed myself to the point that I overdosed or something. Who knows? I'm just so grateful that she decided she was worth it, and she remembered why she was here, which is to make a difference.

How can people become their own success story?

I know I'm going to sound like a broken record, but it's about giving yourself permission, reminding yourself that you're allowed and understanding what your own barometers to success are. Some people might say having a million-dollar business means you're successful, but that's not my barometer. For me, being successful means waking up and feeling refreshed, happy and loved, and being able to do the things I love. Understanding your own barometer for success and happiness, is really important, because it's easy to get caught up in the mind loop of comparing yourself to others and what you think you *should* be doing, until you lose sight of who you are and what your meaning is.

When you do what you love, your performance can't help but elevate.

On a practical level, I help people to become their own success story through my coaching and Whole Body Approach.

Physical: Your Body is Also Your Subconscious.
Reconnect with your body by understanding the impact your brain, nervous system and cellular function have on your results.
Did you know that your cellular body has a set point that needs to be raised, or it will continually create sabotage in your life?

Mental: Your Thoughts Create Frequency.
When you identify your values and beliefs, and harness the shadow side of those values, your internal inspiration expands.
Values and beliefs are formed in childhood, so ask yourself if they now serve you as an adult. For many people it doesn't, but how do you transform them?

Emotional: Feelings Drive Actions.
Identify the feelings that trigger undesirable responses, and clear the emotional blockages from your body that create negative patterns in your life.
This allows more impactful actions and emotions to take place.

Metaphysical: The Powerful Connector.
By embracing the metaphysical and connecting to the immutable universal laws of nature, you're able to harness your thoughts, emotions and actions for a faster outcome and higher level of performance.
Science now proves what the spiritual community always knew.

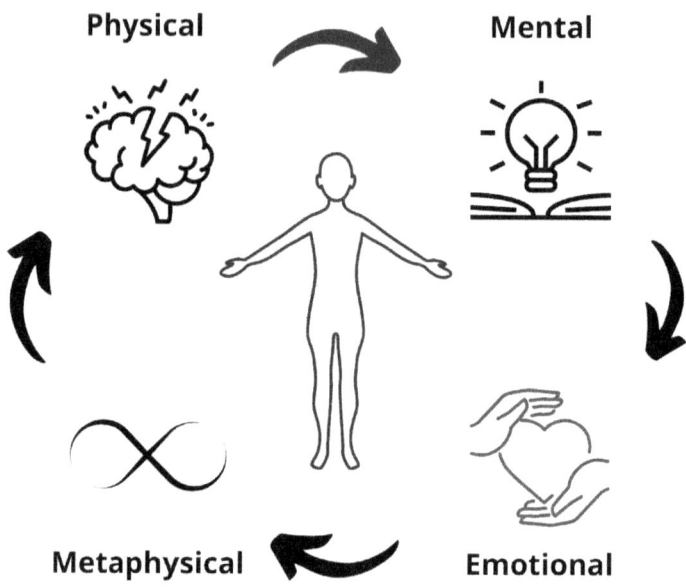

By connecting all the elements of the Whole Body Approach, you can easily increase your performance and attract more wealth, love and happiness into your life.

You raise your frequency to receive while changing the thoughts and emotions that have previously blocked you from having all you truly desire to live your best life.

You truly can have it all.

 To discover more about how Trudi can help you *Elevate Your Performance*, simply visit www.elevatebooks.com/performance

Carole Gibbons
Rapid Results

Carole Gibbons is a certified results coach, yoga and meditation teacher, international best-selling author and Reiki master. She has a great interest in understanding human behaviour, along with an earnest desire to help people identify, clarify and achieve their goals.

Her decades-long systems engineering career has facilitated a detailed and thorough approach to coaching.

Carole uses scientific and spiritual principles to aid clients in identifying and understanding the action steps required to move towards their heart's desire.

Using the power of mindset, Carole has enabled her clients to reach their highest potential and peak performance. She fosters their resilience, so they can flourish, no matter what life throws at them.

Carole Gibbons

Rapid Results

What is the biggest life lesson you've learned?

My biggest life lesson is that the cultivation of resilience allows you to deal with whatever experiences, good or bad, come your way. What I mean by resilience is an individual's capacity to overcome adversity and unpleasant or difficult events, while also being able to adapt to change and uncertainty.

Research shows that resilience is a temporary trait. With training, we can increase our bandwidth or range of resilience, as well as our window of tolerance. It's a state of the autonomic nervous system that puts us in an optimal arousal zone. All learning, change and growth happens here. Increasing our resilience allows us to function more effectively and perform well over a greater range of conditions.

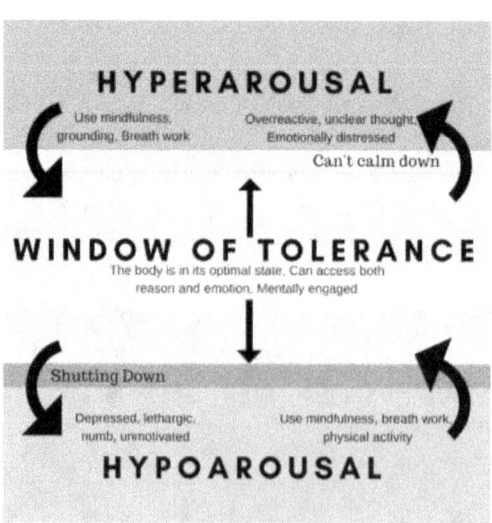

© Richard Bamford Therapy

Negative self-talk can often sabotage our efforts and stop us from leading a happy and fulfilling life. Becoming aware of your self-talk is the very first step in changing your attitude, actions, emotions and vibration, and hence your outcome.

We all vibrate at particular frequencies that change depending on our mindset, thoughts, emotions, words and actions, but we can make a conscious choice to increase our vibration and move away from negative thoughts.

Our vibrations differ from moment to moment, day to day. Imagine the different vibrations equated to floors in a multi-story building. The slower, darker vibrations such as despair, anger and fear live in the basement. Shame and guilt might reside in slightly higher floors, along with disappointment, frustration, unhappiness and sadness. Even higher floors would contain optimism, hope, joy, fulfilment, love, peace, appreciation, gratitude and contentment. In fact, all of the positive emotions. Now visualise that you're an elevator travelling up and down, and you can stop at any floor for as long or as short a time as you want to. The important thing is that you are the elevator and not the floor. You're in control.

Personal development and being coached enables us to change our vibration and make it easier to automatically reside in the more positive floors/emotions, while rarely visiting the lower, darker ones. If we find ourselves at times in a lower vibrational state, we will have learned the skills and actions required to increase our vibration and move to the happier, more positive upper floors once again. But you should know that indulging in drugs, alcohol, binge eating and similar activities, shoots your elevator downwards faster than just about anything else. Practices such as meditation and mantra rewire your brain to naturally become happier and more positive.

We can also use our imagination to re-wire our brains, so that we mainly live in the upper vibrational regions. We can visualise living in the moment of the wish fulfilled. It's possible to raise our vibration and attract our wishes towards us as we think about and visualise our wish/want already fulfilled. We'll see opportunities to achieve our wish and take actions based on these opportunities, which moves us ever closer to our goals.

I suggest spending the first and last five minutes of every day using imagination/visualisation to practise how you would live your life if your wish/goal was already achieved. What would you be seeing, feeling, thinking, experiencing and doing? Would you have an overwhelming sense of appreciation? Then practise that appreciation and gratitude right now by feeling it within yourself as you live in the moment of your wish fulfilled.

If you were speaking to your younger self, what advice would you give?

Don't take yourself too seriously.

Make time for more fun, laughter and happiness.

Don't wait for everything to be perfect in your life before deciding to be happy.

Be confident in your interactions with other people, speak your mind and play full out. Don't hide behind shyness, being reserved or thinking that your thoughts and ideas won't be as good as other people's, or that you won't be appreciated for your innate worth.

Open up, and be more vulnerable. It's worth the risk and leads to much deeper relationships.

Don't be so self-critical, especially about your appearance. This is how you appear to the world, and many people love you just as you are.

How would you like to be remembered?

I would like to be remembered as someone who was always optimistic, helpful and caring, whether it was through my coaching, yoga and meditation, technical advice or practical help with issues.

What's the worst thing that's ever happened to you, and how did you overcome it?

In recent years, the worst thing I experienced was being told my husband, Kelvin had only three to four months to live. This news came virtually out of the blue, and I was totally stunned and numb.

In early 2018, Kelvin had been unwell and had started coughing up blood, which is never a good sign. X-rays and scans showed he had some thickening in his lungs, so he went into hospital for a bronchoscopy, a day surgery, in order to get a biopsy taken and receive a proper diagnosis.

I left him at the hospital in good spirits, but only a couple of hours later I received a phone call telling me that the surgeon wanted to speak with me and to please come back right away. I remember nothing about driving back to the hospital other than feeling terrified that Kelvin was dead.

When I got to the hospital, I was ushered into a room where the consultant told me Kelvin had lung cancer and had three to four months to live. Even worse was that Kelvin's lungs had collapsed during the bronchoscopy, and he was now in the process of being stabilised while on a ventilator in the intensive care unit. I was also introduced to a spiritual care assistant who stayed with me as I tried to process the news. I rang our daughter to tell her and a few hours later was allowed to visit Kelvin in ICU. It was a total shock to see him so still and seemingly lifeless, with a machine breathing for him and tubes everywhere.

Going home alone that evening, I was on automatic pilot, my mind in a spin. I realised that I had to stay strong and focussed for everyone's sake, including mine. Deep inside, I knew that I needed to control what I could, like my reactions and actions, and influence what I was able to influence, such as getting the best treatment for Kelvin. It was important to try my best not to get disturbed by the things that I didn't have any control over.

Over the next few days, I drew upon my many years of practising yoga, pranayama and meditation, to try and calm my mind, while working out what needed to be done on a practical basis. This included ensuring that I was at the ICU every day during ward round time, so I could find out what treatment Kelvin was receiving and how he was progressing. I also talked to my health insurance company to make sure we were covered and informed my employer I wouldn't be able to work full time for a while. But the most upsetting part of all was letting family and friends know of the situation. I had a really hard time dealing with their sympathy. It made me cry and feel powerless.

During the next few weeks, I dug deep and realised that I was actually quite resilient. I was dealing reasonably well with the stress by using meditation and breathing practices to quiet my mind and also utilised my personal values and strengths to regulate my emotions as best I could. I stayed positive and focussed, maintained perspective and tried to remain healthy. The practical and emotional support of our daughter, Amber, really helped.

After ten days, Kelvin was taken off the ventilator and could breathe on his own. It was such a relief. But unfortunately, his brain was pretty scrambled for a few days, and we thought he might have brain damage due to the lack of oxygen when his lungs collapsed. However, his mental alertness and concentration did improve, which was a massive relief.

Even better, a second bronchoscopy, undertaken while he was on the ventilator, did manage to get some tissue samples, and the diagnosis was that he didn't have lung cancer. However, they now had no idea what was actually wrong or why his lungs collapsed. So even though the immediate health crisis was over, when he was discharged from the hospital two weeks later, he'd lost an enormous amount of weight and muscle mass, and could hardly walk. Apparently, this is normal after being on a ventilator for so long, but we were totally unprepared for him to be so weak, and in need of constant care for quite some time.

While all of this was happening, my eighty-five-year-old mum in the UK was in and out of hospital with COPD, and her health was failing fast. My sister, Susan, was keeping me informed, and I could ring mum and have a chat, but I felt so guilty for not being able to visit mum to say goodbye and support my sister on a day-to-day basis.

Once I knew Kelvin didn't have lung cancer, and was starting to slowly recover, I prayed that mum would hang on a bit longer, so Kelvin would be well enough to allow me to go to England for her funeral. It turns out he was discharged by the time mum died, and Amber volunteered to look after him, even though she had a young baby. This allowed me to fly to England to help my sister organise the funeral and say my goodbyes.

After a few months, Kelvin had recovered some of his strength, when he started to feel very ill again, but we thought he had the flu. He had night sweats, he wasn't eating or drinking and generally felt awful. I took him to the GP for a blood test and again got a phone call, this time saying to take him to A&E immediately, as he was in kidney failure.

Carole Gibbons

This started the next round of Kelvin's health issues. He was admitted, and within two days, had a permanent catheter inserted into the blood vessels in his neck that allowed him to receive dialysis. He was told that if he didn't have it, he would be dead within five days.

The kidney failure at least allowed the cause of his various health issues to be identified. He had two autoimmune conditions that had wreaked havoc on his body in their efforts to kill him, first attacking his lungs, causing major bleeding from his sinuses, before moving on to destroying his kidneys and affecting his corneas. Plasma exchanges to remove the antibodies, coupled with six months of chemotherapy, eliminated the autoimmune conditions and eventually allowed him to get on the kidney transplant waiting list.

That was three years ago, and Kelvin is still on dialysis every other day as he waits for a donor kidney. We're now doing haemodialysis at home, and I'm his carer while also holding down a full-time job that provides our family income.

Fortunately, my employer, Nova Systems, has been very understanding about what's going on. I would have really struggled without their support and the extra carers and compassionate leave they've allowed. Long-term illness and being the carer for a loved one who's sick and physically weak, have their own stresses. I'm still actively building my resilience, so I'm able to cope with all that life has brought my way over the last few years.

I firmly believe the universe doesn't send anything your way that you can't handle, and I try my best to use the experiences, reactions and ways of dealing with what I'm going through, as part of my personal development process. I'm still finding that meditation, chanting, being optimistic and regularly counting my blessings allows me to thrive under somewhat difficult circumstances. Since becoming a results coach, I've also found that receiving coaching regularly has helped to remove emotional blocks and limiting beliefs. I'm discovering the wisdom hidden within all of life's experiences, good and bad.

What decisions have made a difference in your life?

In relatively recent years, the biggest decision Kelvin and I made that caused a major difference in our lives, was to emigrate from the UK to Australia. Kelvin had lived in Adelaide and Perth for a year or so when he was travelling the world in his late teens/early twenties, and loved the lifestyle and the people.

Being patriotic at the time, he didn't take out Australian citizenship; so many years later when he wanted to return here to live, he couldn't get permanent residency. He finally managed to persuade me to give it a go, as I'm a professional engineer and qualified for a skills-based visa. But since I was in my fifties at the time, the visa was not an easy process and took a couple of years to actually arrive in Adelaide with a job offer. Our daughter Amber, who was sixteen at the time, was kicking and screaming all the way that we'd ruined her life by uprooting her from her friends.

Despite basically speaking the same language, the culture shock was surprisingly large, so it took a while to settle down and start enjoying the lifestyle.

We were lucky that there were lots of ex Brits in my workforce, so I had help in adapting, fitting in and understanding the Aussie way of doing things. The big things we missed were family and friends, although frequent phone calls to my parents and other close family members helped enormously and reduced homesickness.

Another decision that made a difference was to start investing. In the UK, I hadn't really come across everyday people who invested in property or the stock market., whereas here in Australia it seemed normal and almost commonplace.

Kelvin and I completed a number of training courses on how to wisely invest in property and purchased some investment properties. Then I got around to investing in myself and began a series of personal development training courses, the vast majority with Authentic Education. These were enlightening and satisfied a hunger within me to know myself better. The coaching training course was superb. It made me realise that I'd finally found my life calling, which was being a results coach. I've always enjoyed helping people, but apart from yoga and meditation, it was in an informal, untrained way.

After completing the coaching training, I realised that I now had the tools and expertise to help people in a much more structured way. This eventually led me to setting up my coaching business, Coached by Carole, and beginning my journey of fulfilment via service.

What's the best thing that has ever happened to you, and why?

Having our daughter, Amber, is the best thing that's ever happened to me. She's expanded my horizons in so many ways. She's grown into a beautiful, caring young woman who's provided us with two young grandsons. They're a blessing, full of energy, fun and mischief! They keep me on my toes, and I enjoy every minute of it. They're a true blessing in my life.

What is your big WHY?

My big WHY is my family. In the north of England where I was born and raised, familial closeness was so important. We knew our great aunties and uncles, as well as our first, second and third cousins, and met up regularly for family reunions. Even after they'd emigrated to Canada many years earlier, we kept in touch with relatives and visited as their families grew through the generations. Caring for each other when needed was expected and selflessly provided, and we always celebrated the good times together.

After we moved to Australia, I remember feeling guilty when my stepdad, Colin, was sick, and my sister Susan visited and nursed him every day until he died. She was the one organising the medical appointments and taking him to hospital. The same happened when our mum was terminally ill. My contribution was to phone her regularly to provide a listening ear and an independent viewpoint. I allowed her to talk through her worries and frustrations with the medical system and supported her the very best way I could from such a distance.

Now that Amber and her partner Brandon have two small boys here in Adelaide, I support them without thought and would sacrifice just about anything to provide what they need. It's wonderful to spend happy times with her four-year-old. I'm creating a lasting relationship with him, and the same will be true when her new baby is old enough to form close personal relationships. At the moment, this is limited to lots of cuddles and the offer to babysit. To me, excellent family relationships are the most important thing in my life and are dearly cherished.

Do you have an approach to your results coaching?

I follow a five-step process known as the Rapid Results Model, created by Benjamin J Harvey from Authentic Education. This is exactly what I was taught during my results coaching training. It's proven to be an extremely effective model for empowering people, improving performance and getting great results. It bridges the gap between where you are and where you want to be.

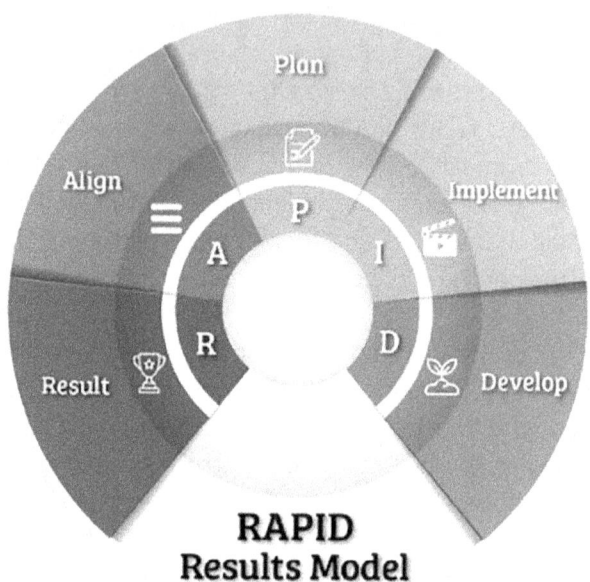

© Authentic Education

R.A.P.I.D. stands for Result, Align, Plan, Implement and Develop.

Result

With the help and guidance of a coach, the client discovers their WHY, realising the new identity they want to move towards and the action steps required. They can then clarify this result and become certain of their path. The hindbrain doesn't like uncertainty, as it doesn't feel safe and procrastinates/sabotages actions towards any goal that's uncertain. Quieting the hindbrain allows detailed, specific goals to be identified and develops timeframes that are achievable, so the client consciously knows the reasons why they want this goal and the first few action steps towards achieving it.

Align

Alignment is achieved through the meaning we place on our experiences. This consists of our values, beliefs, memories, decisions and behaviour patterns, and their meanings may be empowering, neutral or disempowering.

A coach helps the client achieve empowering meanings, which leads to greater action towards their clearly articulated goals. Identifying the client's values and resolving value conflicts, also fall into the align area. In addition, it encompasses overcoming limiting beliefs and eliminating trapped emotions that are affecting your mindset and emotions, which leads to little or no action towards achieving your hopes, dreams and goals.

Asking and answering high-quality questions, and utilising various coaching tools and techniques, ensures the alignment of the client to their goals. The end result is a vastly improved probability of the client taking the required steps and actions.

Plan

The plan stage involves creating systems and processes that the client will use on their journey to reaching their goals, and potentially continue to utilise for the rest of their lives. Understanding the fundamentals, and progressing step by step while learning and consolidating the required skills, gives them expertise and allows continued growth.

Implement

In order to create your desired life, you need to regularly ask yourself some important questions:

1. What actions should I stop doing?

2. What actions should I start doing?

3. What actions should I do less of?

4. What actions should I do more of?

Implement the answers to these questions to hone your skills and apply the actions steps required, so you can realise the life that you've always wanted.

Develop

The purpose of this stage is to develop the client's independence, so that they can achieve success and no longer require the services of a coach.

> "The Result of Your Life=Attitude x Effort x Ability"
> ~ Dr Kazuo Inamori

This equation basically means that the outcome of your work life is a product of attitude, effort and ability. The scores in each of these fields are multiplied together. Attitude is scored from -100 to +100, while effort and ability are scored from 0 to 100. Once you figure out your score, you will realise that your attitude has the greatest effect on your results in life.

> "Your attitude, not your aptitude, will determine your altitude. You will get all you want in life, if you help enough other people get what they want."
> ~ Zig Ziglar

How did you decide on the name and logo for your business?

It came to me as I woke up one morning. I loved the simplicity and alliteration, as well as it stating exactly what my business does. My daughter is very artistic, so I asked her to produce my logo and was blown away by her results. I love the clasped hands in the shape of a heart, signifying a heart-centred business. I felt it depicted how I help my clients elevate their performance by providing accountability, guiding them towards their goals and supporting them as they overcome hurdles, so they can complete the action steps that will lead them to success and achieving their heart's desires.

Is meditation or mindfulness something everyone should practise?

In my experience, definitely. Meditation can take many forms, but the key part is to find a meditation practice that gels with you. It needs to clear away the mist and uncertainty that surrounds you and make you feel good. Some of the benefits of meditation include

- reduced anxiety and depression

- greater resilience to stress

- more energy

- reduced risk of heart attack and stroke

- increased brain function and creativity

- achieving better, more restful sleep.

During meditation, the body experiences a state of profound rest that goes much deeper than the deepest part of the normal sleep cycle. In this state, the body dispels the impact of tension and stress. Meditation also has a measurable effect on brain function. There's an increase in brain coherence, and regular practise of meditation helps rewire the brain's physical connections previously damaged by exposure to trauma and stress.

Consistent practice, even over short timescales, has been found to reduce activity in the brain's amygdala, the collection of cells near the base of the brain that consists of two parts, one in each hemisphere. The amygdala helps coordinate responses to your environment, especially things that trigger an emotional response. It also plays an important role in fear and anger.

Biologically, fear is an important emotion. It helps you respond appropriately to threatening situations that could hurt you. The fear response is generated by stimulation of the amygdala, followed by the hypothalamus, which initiates the fight-or-flight response. The amygdala also plays a role in fear learning, such as the process by which you develop an association between certain situations and feeling fear.

Consistent meditation practice can result in reduced activity in the amygdala while viewing negative images, thus reducing emotional responses to negative stimuli.

In addition to meditation, practising many of the various forms of yoga such as hatha yoga asanas and pranayama on a regular basis, will also result in stress reduction and a healthier response to the negative influences we're exposed to.

Mindfulness and meditation are often used interchangeably, which can be confusing, especially as mindfulness meditation is one of the many forms of meditation!

Mindfulness, as its name suggests, is being aware, noticing and paying attention to thoughts, feelings, actions and everything else. Mindfulness can be practised any time, irrespective of what we're doing or who we're with. It means being fully engaged in the present moment, with no thoughts about the past or the future. There's no judgement, no what ifs and no destructive self-criticism or analysis.

When practising mindfulness, we're totally present, without any distractions. Mindfulness releases endorphins in the brain, which make us feel happy, lowers blood pressure and reduces pain, all beneficial outcomes for just paying attention.

The practice of mindfulness also supports meditation.

Meditation is usually practised for a set amount of time, often in seclusion or a specific meditation area of your home. Some forms are aimed at increasing compassion, loving kindness or forgiveness, while others are for achieving focus and clarity of mind. Some use sound, such as chanting or mantra, or specific breath practices.

During my yoga teacher training, my instructor always told us to practise meditation for the sake of the practice and not to achieve any preconceived or previously experienced outcome. This is so important, as is regularity and consistency of the practice.

What is one thing someone could do now to change their life?

Make a decision to change something in your life for the better right now, and take action.

These are some of the areas that may be blocking you from living your best life:

- Heartbreak over a broken relationship.
- Feeling trapped in your career.
- Lack of motivation.
- Fear of public speaking.
- Being totally stressed out.
- Lack of a deep spiritual connection.
- Addictive behaviour.
- Experiencing a work/life imbalance.
- Hanging on to a failing business.
- Needing to lose weight or improve your health.
- Difficulty sleeping.
- Difficulty communicating with your spouse or children.
- Lack of time to get everything done.
- An inability to pay the bills.

Choose an area of your life that you want to change and the direction you want to head towards. The wheel of life diagram below shows the main aspects of life, but they may be different for you.

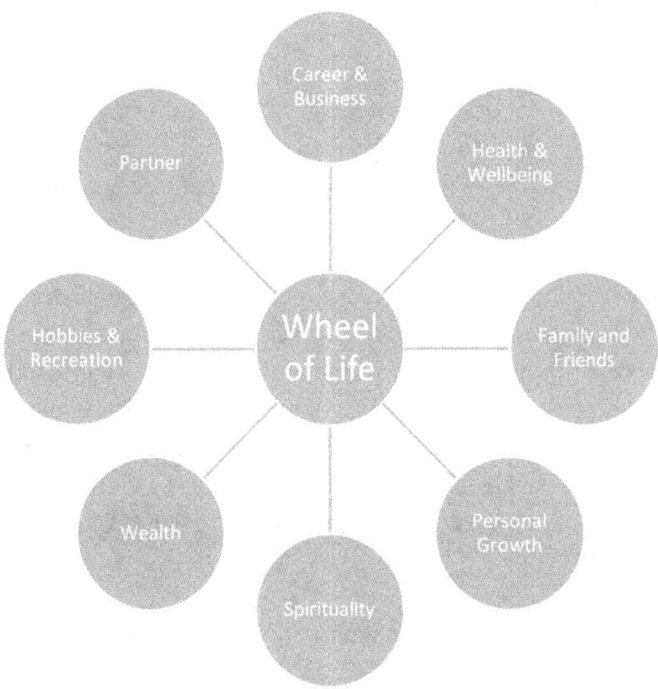

Wheel of Life

We learn from the people we associate with. Initially, it's our families, school friends and teachers. When we become adults and get a job, we continue to associate with people who are similar to us in many ways. In order to achieve new goals or aspirations, you need to be introduced to new thoughts and ideas and choose to modify your behaviours. You can acquire these new concepts through books, documentaries and films. However, the most direct way is by connecting with people who have achieved what you aspire to in the area of life you want to change or improve.

Become the bottom of a group/triangle that consists of those who are more successful, more spiritual, wealthier, happier and healthier than you currently are. By associating with these new people and following their examples, you can modify your own actions and behaviours.

As you practise these new skills, you will rise towards the apex of each group/triangle that you're a member of, and other people may then begin mirroring your actions towards success. In order to continue moving forward, join higher and higher groups associated with each of the different aspects of your life you want to change.

You may find that you start to lose old friends as your paths diverge, because your energies change. For some people, the idea of losing friends or becoming distant from family members causes them to remain where they are, even though they're dissatisfied with their lives and may lack the motivation or courage to move forward. However, there's always a chance that at some stage they'll choose to move towards their own success, even if some pain or loss is associated with this transformation.

Why do you think people are working in a job they dislike?

I suspect that it's because they don't know what else to do. Growing up, their examples and role models worked at jobs they didn't like, just to pay for rent, food or clothing for their families. This would have been true for whole neighbourhoods, not just their own family. Until we become aware that we have choices and start making conscious decisions about our actions, we will continue to unconsciously model the behaviour that we're familiar with from childhood or early adulthood.

Do you recommend any spiritual practices to keep you or your clients at their peak?

I'm currently enjoying mantra meditation. My husband and I recently attended a course on Nada Yoga, or the Yoga of Sound, and thoroughly enjoyed it. We then followed this up with a forty-day practice of repeating a mantra we'd each chosen, which brought more discipline into our daily lives. We both made sure we did our chanting practice every day, sometimes more than once.

As a trained yoga and meditation teacher, I would definitely recommend a daily practice of some sort, whether it be asana (yoga poses), pranayama (breath work), meditation practice or something else that inspires you. It doesn't need to take much time. Start with five minutes, and progress to fifteen or thirty minutes daily. The most important thing is to find something that resonates with you. This can take some trial and error, until you find just the right one. Over time, of course, this can change as you evolve and open up your perception to more types of inspiration or creativity in your life.

 To discover more about how Carole can help you *Elevate Your Performance*, simply visit www.elevatebooks.com/performance

Marty Hassan
Unlocking High Performance

Marty is a high-performance coach, trainer and consultant, who's partnered with emerging and established leaders in some of the world's most prominent companies in their field. His mission is to embrace their potential, create positive impact in others, and achieve step-change results through their people.

In his pursuit to master his coaching and intervention techniques, Marty sought out the world's best peak-performance specialists to mentor him.

Marty has partnered with thousands of leaders in Fortune 100 companies across industries, from oil and gas to aerospace. He's helped them bring out the best in their employees and save their businesses millions of dollars in the process.

Today, Marty directly impacts many lives with his leadership and mindset products, live events and coaching programs.

Marty Hassan

Unlocking High Performance

What is your definition of high performance?

If you ask people to define high performance, you're likely to get different answers and contexts.

My first experience of observing high performance came when I was only eighteen years old. I grew up in Ireland and was fanatical about hurling, a team sport played with a wooden stick (a hurley) and a small ball (a Sliotar). I started playing at the under 12 level. My first coach was a tall man named Liam, who had an enormous physical and energetic presence. He was a retired teacher, articulate and direct with his words, and a great storyteller. When he yelled instructions during training sessions, you listened.

He had two sons on the team, both great friends of mine. My lasting memory is the monotony of practising the basic skills over and over again at every training session. My team was successful throughout the years and won the county championship at every age level. When I played in the under 18 team, we won the county and provincial championships, and were about to compete for a chance to win the under 18 All-Ireland Championship.

A men's county team, Kilkenny, had won eight out of ten All-Ireland Championships throughout that decade. By chance, my coach was from Kilkenny, and as part of our preparation for the most important game of our lives, he took my team there to attend a training session. I was so excited to see my idols, that I couldn't sleep. As we travelled on the bus to the stadium, I remember asking myself what the best team in the country did differently to be the greatest and was full of anticipation for my question to get answered.

When we arrived at the stadium, my teammates and I stood at the side-line as the Kilkenny players emerged from the tunnel and got into position for their first drill. I noticed that it was the exact one our coach had been using since I was twelve. The Kilkenny players then moved into their second, third and fourth drill, all of which were also the same!

I turned to my coach and asked him, "The best team in the country trains the exact same way we do. They're doing nothing but practising the basic skills?" My coach turned to me, paused with a knowing smile and said: "When you practise the basics with discipline and consistency, you'll be world-class".

I didn't realise it at the time, but that one sentence profoundly impacted how I observed high performance and what it takes to achieve it. The three words that stood out for me were 'practise', 'basics' and 'consistency'. Perhaps my coach had studied the famous philosopher, Aristotle, who said:

"Excellence is an art won by training and habituation. We do not act rightly because we have virtue or excellence, but rather have those because we have acted rightly. We are what we repeatedly do. Excellence then is not an act, but a habit".

How do people achieve high performance?

To influence high performance, you must first get clear on your measure of the term. After consulting and coaching in Fortune 100 companies, I've seen an excessive number of key-performance indicators (KPIs) posted on office walls and in company reports. The majority of organisations gauge their success on outcomes and results, which comes as no surprise, since the core outputs of most businesses can be measured using quantity, time or some derivative of the two.

In my early career, I was a mechanical engineer. I spent a lot of time conducting root-cause analyses of failure modes in fighter jet engines and applied these principles of cause and effect to high performance.

Sir Isaac Newton, considered one of the most prominent scientists of all time and a major figure in the scientific revolution, formulated three simple laws of motion. In his third law, he states that for every action, there's an equal and opposite reaction. The laws of behaviour act in a similar manner.

My experience with root-cause analysis takes me to the same conclusion. If high performance results are the effect, then employee behaviours and habits are the cause.

Here's the thing. Low-performance behaviour will create low-performance results, just as easy as high-performance behaviour generates high-performance results.

If managers and supervisors aren't applying the laws of behaviour consciously and correctly, they're almost certainly decreasing some behaviours they want and increasing others they don't. To have sustainable high performance, the one thing executives, managers, and supervisors should understand is human behaviour and how to influence it.

Most managers and leaders know enough about human behaviour to comprehend that positive management approaches are more favoured than negative ones. However, they usually know very little about how the selection, delivery and timing of positive and negative consequences in the workplace can influence the way people behave.

What's the cost of poor performance?

In my almost ten years of consulting and coaching experience, conducting employee engagement surveys and my own personal experience, I've found that employee engagement scores are consistently low across the board. A disengaged workforce means people are doing just enough not to get fired. Studies have shown that the level of effort put in by disengaged employees is around forty percent of their capacity.

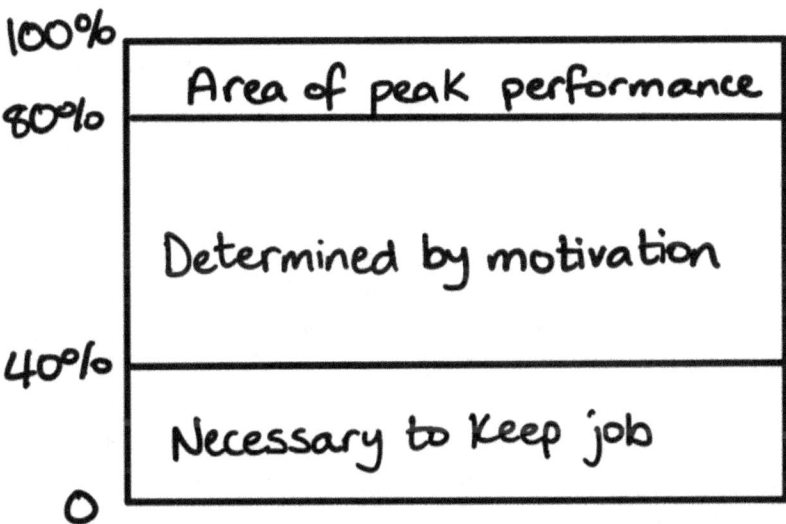

What if they could find a way to tap into the sixty percent discretionary effort that's available? What impact would that have on their results? What would happen if they could access it with consistency and discipline? Could they be world-class?

What is the glue that connects behaviours to results?

Feedback is the single greatest tool leaders have at their disposal for influencing employee behaviour. More specifically, *effective* feedback. It connects the dots between behaviour and consequence.

If you want someone to change, you must connect the current behaviour to its consequences. Imagine you have a child, and they're playing with a ball close to the cooker, and it has a pot of boiling water bubbling on it, so you yell at them to stop playing so close to the cooker. Your child hears the aggression in your voice and immediately stops playing. You're relieved, because you've averted the danger.

But the next day they're back playing by the cooker. Why have they repeated the old behaviour? The answer is because they haven't associated the potential negative consequences of their actions.

Consider what would happen if the conversation had gone something like, "If you play too close to the cooker, you might accidentally hit the pot, and the boiling water will spill all over you, creating pain and scarring you for life."

This may be a pretty extreme example, but you get the idea that you've now connected a negative consequence to the behaviour. If the child doesn't want to feel the pain of burning themselves, they won't play close to the cooker again.

When you master the science of effectively delivering feedback, you move from being a novice to a leader who creates high-performing teams that generate high-performance results.

What are the different types of feedback?

The purpose of giving feedback is to increase the frequency of a behaviour that generates high-performance results and to decrease the behaviours that produce low-performance results.

There are two types of feedback that increase performance. Negative reinforcement creates an environment where people will exert just enough effort to escape or avoid punishment. Positive reinforcement produces discretionary effort, which means they go above and beyond what's expected. Unlocking discretionary effort is the secret to maximising performance in the workplace.

Because reinforcement is defined as any consequence that increases performance, it always works. If performance does not increase after the delivery of a consequence, then by definition, the consequence wasn't a positive reinforcer.

Any kind of punishment or penalty will decrease performance. The most common form of punishment is what I call *obsolescence*. This is when the performer takes an action, and leaders ignore the positive behaviours of their employees, neglecting to recognise or reward them. You know it's occurring when you hear people say, "Nobody appreciates anything I do around here".

In his book *The Power of Habit*, Charles Duhigg defined the habit loop in three steps:

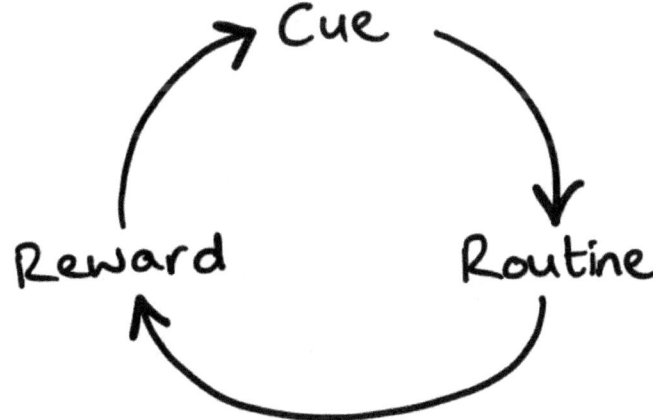

James Clear took this principle and added a critical fourth step in his book, *Atomic Habits*. He defines the habit loop as shown in the graph below:

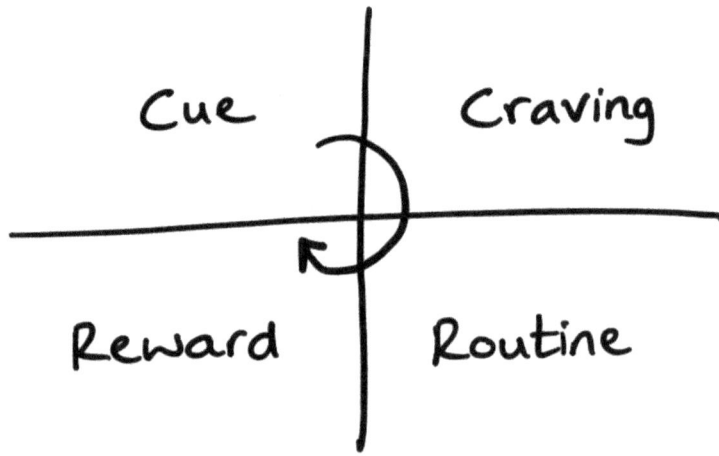

Both of these authors understood the value of emotional reward and how it drives humans. We crave moving from negative to positive emotions.

Take for example the cue of feeling stressed. The craving is to feel relaxed, so let's say the habit is to have a glass of wine. The reward is relaxation. Once the brain finds a behaviour that satisfies the craving and achieves the reward, a new habit is formed.

How does someone change behaviours?

In simple terms, you need to associate pleasure with the behaviours you want to increase, and pain with the behaviours you want to reduce. The cue and craving can stay the same in the equation, but as you change the routine, you must also calibrate the associated reward to increase pain or pleasure.

All you need to do is positively reinforce behaviours associated with high performance. Change the routine to achieve the desired reward, and increase the emotional intensity of the that reward, so the new behaviour is more desirable than the old one.

In the example above, instead of having a glass of wine, what if you exercised? Would you feel an even greater sense of positive emotion? Maybe you'd have a sense of achievement or even joy. If the feeling is more pleasurable than what the glass of wine provides, then you've found a new routine that gives you an even greater emotional reward. You now have the makings of a new habit.

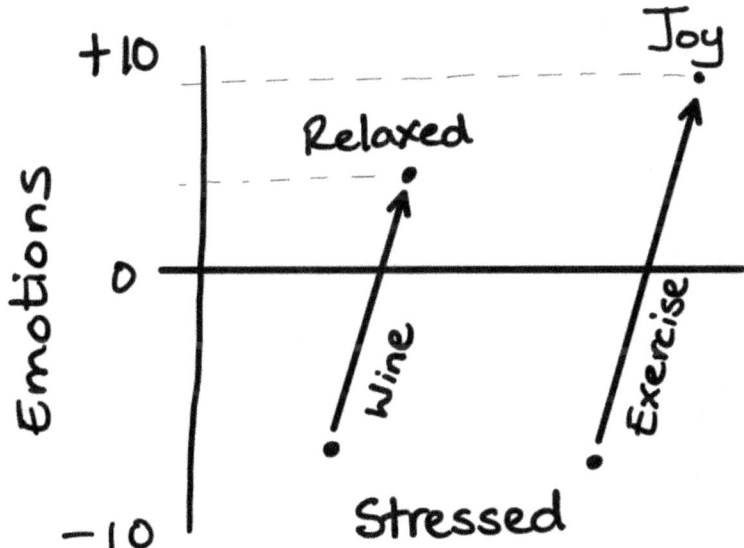

What do you think are the main problems/challenges leaders face in achieving results?

I've been helping leaders create high-performing teams for close to a decade with both my coaching business and High-Performance Leader programs. Over time, I've discovered three core issues leaders come up against when delivering feedback to employees.

1. **Not knowing the correct framework to deliver feedback effectively.**

   Leaders aren't taught how to structure their feedback conversations, so it's not done effectively, and many of the fundamental building blocks of influence are missing, such as not knowing how to

   - plan effectively
   - provide a verbal contract, giving you permission to offer constructive feedback
   - include critical elements like leveraging consequences, agreeing to the new actions, and holding people accountable.

   All of these elements have a catastrophic effect on your feedback being heard and acted upon, and ultimately, your relationship with the receiver.

2. **Lack of time.**

   One of the most common problems leaders have when delivering feedback, especially constructive feedback, is that they don't have time. They're too busy firefighting, trying to get things done, to achieve the results dictated by the business KPIs.

   When I ask them why they're so busy, the most frequent answer I receive is that they're picking up the slack from those who aren't pulling their weight. These leaders are telling me, without realising it, that they're tolerating poor performance and trying to compensate for others by working harder.

3. **Lack of confidence.**

   The third problem, which I actually think is the biggest one of all, is that leaders lack confidence. Many are afraid of having constructive feedback conversations and would do anything to avoid having them, including tolerating poor performance.

When you go out there to solve those problems, you need to

- get structured in your approach to having productive conversations with poor performers
- make sure delivering effective feedback conversations is a priority
- overcome your fear and increase your confidence for having feedback conversations with even the most challenging personnel.

What I know is that if you're well-positioned to bring out the best in your people and leverage your teams to deliver consistently on your commitments, you'll have

- freedom from stress
- the ability to do the things you enjoy
- a real sense of achievement, success and fulfilment.

Why do you think leaders are afraid to have constructive feedback conversations?

Here's what I know after coaching over a thousand leaders and having many of them participate in my workshops on Creating High-Performing Teams with Effective Feedback. I realised that most of them use the word 'conflict' to describe having constructive feedback conversations. These are exact quotes from leaders who've participated:

- "I'm afraid of conflict".
- "I'm afraid of a negative response that might lead to conflict".
- "Giving feedback will cause confrontation and conflict".
- "The other person has an argumentative attitude, and it will end in conflict".
- "The last time I tried to give feedback, it negatively impacted the relationship".

It's interesting that the word conflict comes from the Latin words 'con', which means 'together', and 'fligere', which is 'to strike'. Combined, they create the word 'configere', or 'a striking together', meaning 'to be in opposition, or at variance'.

In the early fifteenth century, it evolved in old French to mean 'armed encounter or battle'. By 1743, the phrase 'conflict of interests' was in frequent use.

The goal of having any kind of feedback conversation should be to

- bring out the best in every member of your team
- help them become an even better version of themselves
- grow and add more value to the relationship.

My belief is that with this goal in mind, having constructive conversations is akin to offering someone a gift.

Imagine a time in the past when someone offered you a present you cherished. How did it make you feel to receive it? Appreciated? Connected? Valued? Validated? How about a time when you put lots of thought into getting a gift for someone close to you. How did you feel when you offered it and saw the appreciation in their eyes when they received it? I know from experience that it's one of the best feelings in the world.

If you intend to help someone sincerely, then I invite you to challenge yourself. Anytime your thoughts begin to focus on conflict when you plan a constructive conversation, instead refocus on the principle that you're offering the recipient the gift of growth.

This single belief, the association of conflict with constructive conversations, is a major block to having them.

What's the biggest mistake you've made in the area of delivering constructive feedback?

Twelve years ago, I made a decision to transition from my engineering role into my first leadership position. I became the operations manager for a joint venture company that manufactured helicopter engines. I was stressed and overwhelmed, drowning in an ocean of work. I had an overwhelming need to prove myself to my boss, so I said yes to every request, no matter how unreasonable.

I was so afraid to provide feedback to my boss about the way he was making me feel by loading me up with more work than I could handle, because I didn't want to be perceived as a failure, so I kept quiet. How did that serve me? My health suffered. I was working so much, I started eating junk food, since it was quick and easy. I stopped socialising with friends, gave up playing for my football team, and my partner left me. I got to my breaking point, so the only way I knew how to deal with the problem was to run away from it. I took a career break and travelled the world.

Along that journey, I made a decision and took action in the form of learning everything I could about leadership, mindset and the art of delivering effective feedback. Six years ago, I joined a consulting business where I had two key objectives. The first was to give feedback to leaders with the single goal of helping them improve their performance. The second was to help them bring out the best in their employees by teaching the leaders how to deliver effective feedback on a daily basis.

The first three weeks of that job were the scariest of my life. I felt the fear of potential judgement and failure bubbling up once again. But I practised everything I learned on strengthening my mindset and stepped into what I would call a stretch zone that helped me authentically deliver feedback to the leaders I was working with. Since then, I've been honoured to help hundreds of leaders master the craft of effective feedback and bring out the best in their employees, while creating high-performing teams.

So what was my biggest mistake in the area of delivering constructive feedback? Delaying my leadership journey due to fear. If I'd said something when I first realised I was taking on too much, I would never have gotten to breaking point. My lesson is the inspiration for this chapter. I want to make sure you have the courage to have feedback conversations when you need to, so you can learn from my mistakes without having to go on a similar journey.

Why do people react negatively to critical feedback?

When we associate with the idea that we're in conflict with others, we fear failure, being rejected by our peers and ultimately being alienated from our tribe.

Let's go back to the evolution of humans. One unique trait is that we have a brain that's six-seven times larger than other mammals of similar weight. In homo sapiens, the brain consumes twenty-five percent of the body's energy when it's at rest, even though it only makes up about two-three percent of our total body weight. Compare this to the brains of other apes, which consume only eight percent of the body's energy when at rest.

Prehistoric humans paid for their large brains in two ways. The first was spending more time searching for food to fuel it. The second was that their muscles atrophied energy, because it was being redirected to their brains.

Another uniquely human trait is that we walk upright on two legs, making it easier to scan the savannah for food or enemies. It also freed up our arms for other purposes, like developing sophisticated tools. But there is a downside to walking. Standing upright and supporting a large head required narrower hips, which had a more significant impact on women, as it restricted the birth canal just as babies' heads were getting bigger. Women who gave birth early were more likely to survive, because the heads were still small.

As a result, human babies are born more prematurely compared with other animals. Human babies are helpless and entirely dependent on their elders for food, protection and education. A lone mother would find it difficult to forage for enough food for her and her child, so she required constant support from other family members and neighbours.

This was the beginning of the formation of tribes. Natural selection consequently favoured those capable of forming strong social ties that built trust and added value to the tribe. They created a trusting and safe space where the members worked together to protect themselves from predators.

The tribal nature of humans was one of the most critical mechanisms for survival, which developed a strong need for connection and acceptance. Being collaborative meant you were trusted and accepted, making you safe from outside dangers. If you found you no longer trusted or were in conflict with members of the tribe, you could be considered an enemy. You'd be judged, rejected and alienated, thus putting your very survival at risk.

When you feel like you will be alienated from the tribe, your survival instincts kick in, and the fight-or-flight response is triggered. When you're in survival mode, the only goal is protecting yourself. It requires complete selfishness, where all you can think about is you.

How does this relate to the business world?

When you've been given constructive feedback that highlights the negative consequences of your behaviours, you may try any number of strategies to show you're still valuable to your tribe or team. You feel like you need to do whatever it takes to survive.

I've seen employees *blame* others. They try to *deflect* and change the focus of the conversation to someone who's more at fault than they are. They *dismiss* the consequences of their behaviours and do their best to *avoid* the 'telling off'. They try to form *alliances* within the tribe to get people on their side for the anticipated 'conflict'. Ultimately, they're trying to avoid the perceived catastrophic consequences they've created in their minds, which is fear of not surviving.

Do we really respond like Stone-Age people?

In 1972, two evolutionary biologists, Stephen Jay Gould of Harvard University and Niles Eldredge of the American Museum of Natural History, proposed the idea of punctuated equilibrium, which helps us understand better why our genes lag behind changes in society. Their theory suggests that evolution is preceded by long periods of stability.

Historians point out just two punctuation points from hunter-gatherer, Stone-Age society. The first was the move to agriculture and the relatively recent shift to an urban, industrial culture.

The timeline goes like this: around 70,000 years ago, during the cognitive revolution, is when homo sapiens emerged as hunter-gathers living in tribes and developing qualities appropriate to that life. Then, between twelve and seven-thousand years ago, the agricultural revolution occurred, leading to a completely different society. A little over two-hundred years ago, industry and trade began to triumph over agriculture, and life conditions were entirely transformed.

Our environment has changed radically since the Stone Age, but we haven't. Evolutionary psychologists argue that we're hardwired with the same circuits that were functional for tribe-living hunter-gatherers. Why is this the case? Seven-thousand years is not enough time for humans to evolve enough to produce the genetic traits to meet the new environment.

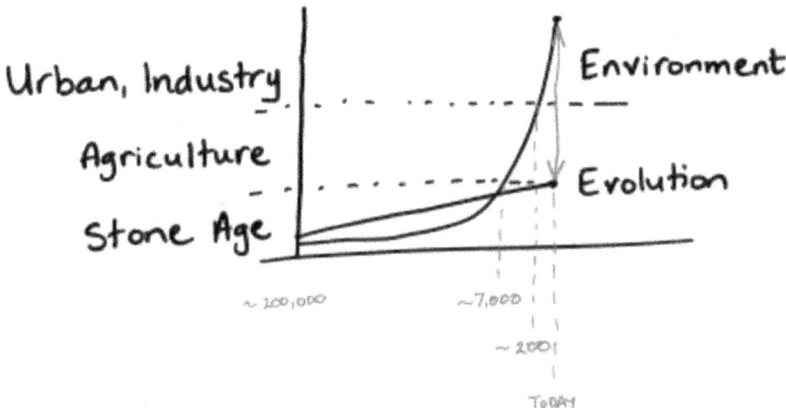

Why does emotion dominate reason?

Evolutionary psychologists say that our emotions take precedence over our reasoning. Good instincts saved lives. Those who passed on more of their genes became honed for survival. Emotions were, and are, the first reaction to everything seen or sensed.

So evolutionary psychologists argue that when we receive feedback, especially if it has a negative element, our natural disposition is not to think about it. Instead, we react emotionally.

Even when we realise it, we're easily influenced, because sincere emotion is so much more important to us than level-headed reason.

How can someone approach a feedback conversation if the science shows that people will respond emotionally?

There are six critical steps to a successful and effective feedback conversation, so the receiver hears it and takes action. They're reflected in the graphic on the next page.

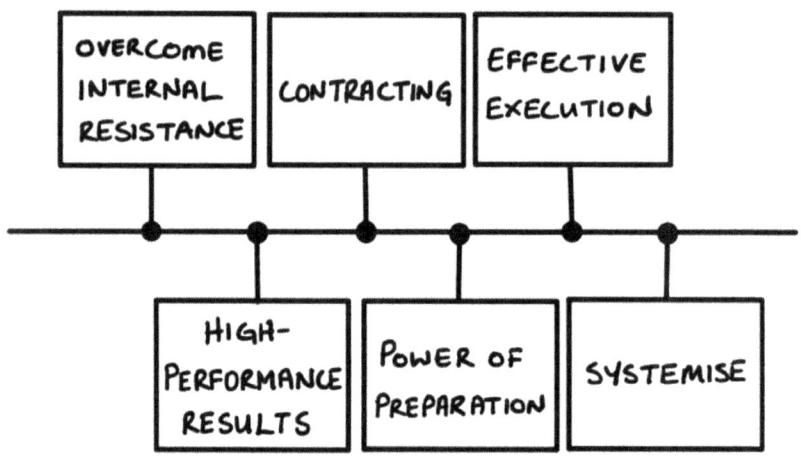

1. **Overcome Internal Resistance**

   Learn how to overcome the fear of having difficult conversations.

2. **High Performance Results**

   Create clarity for the results you want and the behaviours necessary to achieve them.

3. **Contracting**

   Create a verbal contract with the receiver that gives you permission to offer constructive feedback, with the understanding that it will help them grow.

4. **Power of Preparation**

   Systematically prepare for the eight steps of delivering effective feedback to anyone.

- **F -** Foundations
- **E -** Endorsement
- **E -** Execution
- **D -** Diagnosis
- **B -** Begin Empathetic Enquiry
- **A -** Action Plan
- **C -** Contract
- **K -** Kudos

5. **Effective Execution**

    Manage any emotional reactions from the receiver, and keep the conversation on track to get the desired outcome.

6. **Systemise**

    Embed systems into your business that will turn feedback into a daily habit and create a high-performance culture.

How did you learn to regulate your emotions before having a constructive feedback conversation?

The first and most critical step I failed to consider before approaching feedback conversations with my boss, was to regulate my emotions and overcome my internal resistance. The way I discovered how to do this was through a process of vetting my emotions. In other words, I had to make a careful and critical examination of how I was feeling. I've refined the list over the years into the following four questions:

1. **How do I feel right now?**

    Our feelings are the language of the body. When we vet our emotions, we become more aware of them based on how our body responds. How does your body let you know that you're afraid? Maybe you sweat, tremble or get hot flushes or chills. Perhaps you have shortness of breath, a choking sensation, a rapid heart rate, tightness in the chest or butterflies in your stomach. All of these responses are ways you embody an emotion. When you check in with yourself, you can label the feeling with an emotion.

2. **What am I making this conversation mean for me to feel this way?**

    If feelings are the language of the body, the target of your thoughts is the brain's language. The meaning given to events determines the emotions you feel. Imagine you've organised a romantic dinner for you and your partner, and they're an hour late. While you're waiting, you might feel some negative emotions. Maybe it's frustration, anger, resentment or something like deflation. What meaning would you have to give to your partner being late to trigger one or more of those emotions? These are a few examples:

    - "They don't respect me".

    - "They're so inconsiderate".

    - "They don't love me".

    - "Maybe they're cheating on me."

    You can see that any one of these meanings would generate a negative emotional response. But suppose you vet the target of your thoughts. In that case, you become aware that the meaning you give certain events occurs subconsciously and is often based on old conditioning and projecting past experience onto the current situation.

3. **How would I rather feel instead?**

You could get in a more optimal emotional state to get the results you want in any situation. If you're feeling afraid, are you likely to take the same actions you would if you felt confident? I can almost guarantee the answer is no. Psychology tells us that our emotions determine our behaviours, and our actions determine our results, so it makes sense that if you want high-performance results, you must behave in ways that enable you to achieve those outcomes. Using cause-and-effect theory, it's logical to conclude that your emotions determine your actions.

Once you've identified how you're feeling and why you're feeling that way, you then need to ask yourself, *What would be a more resourceful emotion to feel in this moment?*

4. **How can I change how I feel right now?**

Now that you understand you're still wired like your Stone-Age ancestor, where your instincts and emotions trump logic, you also need to remember that you control the meaning you give your experiences and the emotions you feel.

Growing up in Ireland, I remember the shamrock being intertwined with Irish culture. It was introduced by Saint Patrick, the patron saint of Ireland. He made it famous when talking about Christianity by using the shamrock's three leaves to represent the holy trinity of the father, the son, and the holy spirit; which are the consubstantial elements of one God.

In the same way, there are only three elements to any one emotion. The good news is that you can control these to feel any emotion you choose. The goal is to start doing it consciously.

In my workshops, I share with participants the need to consciously V.E.T. your emotions. The word V.E.T has two meanings. The first is from the dictionary, meaning *to make a careful and critical examination*. But it's also an acronym for the three ingredients that make up any emotion you ever feel.

V. Vocabulary (The words you use to describe your experience.)
E. Embodiment (How you use your body to feel the emotion.)
T. Target of attention (What is the target you're focusing your attention on?)

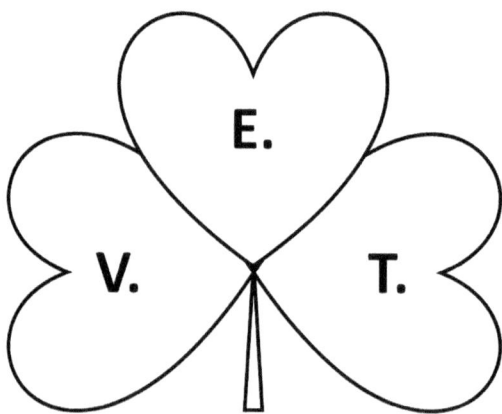

During my workshop, Creating High-Performing Teams with Effective Feedback, I realised that almost every participant answered the first three questions as I did when I originally put myself through this process. My answers in order were

- fear
- it's going to cause conflict
- confident.

To consciously change my emotional state, I had to first become aware of the ingredients that had gone into the recipe for my current emotion.

Here are the ingredients that I added to my recipe of fear.

Vocabulary	Embodiment	Target of Attention
I'm not good enough.	Tension in my shoulders.	Focused on the negatives.
I don't want to do this.	Squeezing my hands.	Not being liked.
I can't do this.	Fidgeting.	How to avoid the conversation.
I'm scared.	Pacing.	Failure and judgement
Is it really worth it?	Hunched (Making myself small.)	They won't respond.
They won't understand.	Shallow, fast breathing.	They will respond aggressively.
Why would they do this?	Sweating.	I will lose respect.
They're idiots.	Feeling hot flushes.	Their negativity will impact the team.

When delivering constructive feedback, the emotion I wanted to have instead of fear was confidence. Below is a list of the V.E.T. ingredients that made up my recipe for confidence.

Vocabulary	Embodiment	Target of Attention
I'm going to nail it.	Shoulders back.	The positive result I want.
I'm bulletproof.	Standing upright.	Connection.
I'm unstoppable.	Smiling.	Being present.
I'm the man/woman.	Chin-up.	Helping others.
I've got this.	Eye contact.	Focus on what works.
I can accomplish anything.	Deep, slow breath.	On the task.
This is easy.	Centred and grounded.	Smashing it.
How good am I?	Relaxed.	Enjoyment.

What's the fastest way you know to change fear into confidence?

I've found that focusing on how I embody an emotion is the quickest and easiest way to change my emotional state. Think about it. How easy is it to stop and take three slow, deep breaths, smile and stand tall? I call it my rapid three, and it's super easy! So if you want to start feeling confident, always begin with your sub-ingredients for Embodiment, and then add in the Vocabulary and Target ingredients.

How can someone influence the emotions of the receiver of the constructive feedback?

Remember that the receiver reacts emotionally. More often than not, the leader delivering the feedback does it in a way that makes the receiver feel threatened and unsafe, which triggers the fight-or-flight response. Your goal as a leader is to help the feedback receiver feel safe and trust in your intentions.

How can someone make the receiver listen to what they're saying?

The way to help them feel safe is to do something called 'pre-frame'. This is a frame of reference that happens before the experience has taken place. For example, suppose I'm about to introduce an activity at a workshop that requires a considerable amount of thought and consideration. In that case, I might say, "We're just about to do an activity that's going to be easy and fun, and will have a hugely positive impact on your performance". In this way, I've directed the participants' expectations and views of the exercise.

Just like a picture frame creates boundaries, the frames of reference a leader chooses as a result of their perspectives can limit them or open up lots of possibilities. Changing the frame can significantly impact how the leader perceives, interprets and responds to an experience.

What is a good pre-frame for receiving feedback without getting defensive?

Not only should you deliver feedback to others to increase their performance, but you also want to receive it in order to grow and develop into an even better leader than you are today.

My experience tells me that a significant amount of people associate feedback with failure. They make it mean that they've done something wrong, and being wrong means they're a failure. If this is where the target of your attention is, what kind of emotional state do you think you would be in? I would guess a pretty unresourceful one.

I know this pattern personally, because this is the frame I created for years. I was so afraid of receiving what I considered criticism of my value and personal worth, I would either defend my actions or dwell in self-pity and self-criticism. It took me a long time to understand a simple truth: this frame is not conducive to increasing my performance!

So I came up with a new frame around feedback and failure. It goes something like this:

- **F.** Feedback
- **A.** Analyse
- **I.** Improve
- **L.** Learn
- **U.** Upgrade
- **R.** Responsibility
- **E.** Expansion
- **S.** Success

F.A.I.L.U.R.E.S. are a gift of **F**eedback that I can **A**nalyse to find opportunities to **I**mprove and **L**earn, so that I can **U**pgrade my skills, take **R**esponsibility for my **E**xpansion, and ultimately be **S**uccessful.

By changing the frame of what failures meant, I now associate them with success. I have a simple visual reminder on the wall of my office:

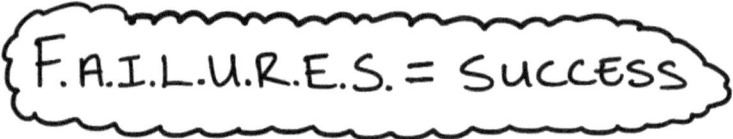

This formula is the epitome of a growth mindset. Dr Carol S. Dweck, in her book *Mindset*, contends that people with a growth mindset find success in doing their best, learning, growing and improving. People with growth mindsets don't mind losing, as long as they see improvement or feel like they've done the best they could.

Your role as a leader is to bring out the best in your people. One of the most powerful leadership tools I know of is delivering feedback effectively and connecting behaviour to consequences.

It's such an under-utilised tool, because your biology often becomes an obstacle for you. Your first step to bringing out the best in yourself and your team is to practise moving from fear to courage. The easiest way to make that transition in a matter of moments is to V.E.T. your emotions and add the ingredients of Courage and Confidence.

Your investment of pre-framing feedback as a gift of improvement, learning and upgrading, so individuals can take responsibility for their expansion and success, will completely shift the receiver's perspective of what feedback is and its intent. You will notice people asking for more feedback to feel the achievement of continuously improving their own and the team's performance. By following these simple steps, you will know that you are well on your way to creating a high-performance environment.

Great leaders who know how to bring out the best in their people is one of the scarcest commodities in the business world. Employees are crying out for great leaders. There has never been a better time for you to step up and start creating a high-performance culture in your team and organisation. I want to sincerely acknowledge your commitment to growth and your desire to serve as a leader at the highest level. I wish you every success in your journey.

 To discover more about how Marty can help you *Elevate Your Performance,* simply visit

www.elevatebooks.com/performance

Irina Castellano

Supported Parenting

Irina Castellano is an authorised foster carer who's dedicated to providing safe homes for vulnerable children.

Her work has been featured in interviews with *SBS German Radio* and *The Meaningful Monday Radio Show*. She also runs the nationally-recognised 'Shared Lives' programs and 'Open Adoption' sessions.

Using her over twenty years of experience, Irina provides awareness and education around all aspects of fostering. She offers professional one-on-one support, training and guidance to all potential foster carers and hopeful adoptive parents.

Along with her husband and three children, Irina has provided a home to over seventy children. Her upcoming memoir will cover the trials, tribulations and joy she's experienced on her foster and adoptive journey.

Irina Castellano
Supported Parenting

If you were speaking to your younger self, what advice would you give?

Trust your gut feeling, follow your dreams and fully embrace life-long learning.

'Everything happens for a reason' is a great motto to live by. Though you might not see the bigger picture and reasoning behind something, it will fall into place at some point in your life.

Have you had any aha moments that changed everything for you?

While living in Statesville, North Carolina in the U.S.A. when I was fifteen years old, I read the book *A Child Called It* by Dave Pelzer. It chronicles Dave's story about how he was brutally beaten and starved by his emotionally unstable, alcoholic mother and how she considered him an 'it'.

Though I'm aware some people have said this is a fictional account, it had a huge impact on me. Having lived a rather privileged-lifestyle as an expat child, I was blown away by how a mother could treat her own child like this.

I'd seen a lot of poverty while travelling, but I'd never heard about child abuse on this level and knew nothing about the fostering system.

What decisions have made a difference in your life?

The best decision I've ever made was not only to marry David, but also that we didn't delay our fostering and adoptive journey.

I'd at least read the book, but David knew nothing about fostering and initially just went along to please his wife, but he's been incredible with each and every child in our home, whether adopted, fostered or biological.

In our home, there's Celina, age seventeen, who we adopted from Singapore during the time we lived there. Then there's Ricky, our biological child, age sixteen, and Madison, twelve, who was locally adopted in NSW, Australia.

Foster children are usually younger than the biological kids in a household, in order to keep the hierarchy. It often works better when they can be guided by the older ones.

All of our kids are quite knowledgeable when it comes to redirecting behavioural issues or emotional outbursts with children from all backgrounds and cultures. They've also become more aware of the effects drugs have on a baby in the womb and what the consequences of a one-night stand may be.

Watching a baby going through withdrawal symptoms (FASD, when the birth-mum consumes alcohol during the pregnancy), or seeing a child suffer when they can't see their parent in jail, are all ways for them to understand certain realities they wouldn't normally be confronted with.

How did your kids come into your life?

We adopted Celina while we were living in Singapore for five years. She was two-and-a-half months old and so tiny when we first met her. It was an incredible feeling knowing we could provide a safe home for her. She was a beautiful baby, and she created our family.

A year later our biological child, Ricky, came into our life, and we thought our family was complete, even though we'd always wanted three kids. But we felt blessed and content.

Once back in Sydney, we continued to foster. Eventually we discovered that one of these children, Madison, wasn't going to be reunited with her birth family, so we were asked if we wanted to keep her permanently or maybe even adopt her. We immediately said yes, but the process of adopting her still took a few years.

Nowadays, the adoption process is supposed to be much faster, as it's been well-documented that kids in care feel a huge relief and sense of security when it becomes official, and it's much more streamlined now.

It should be noted that we appreciate all of our extended family, who were always supportive and inclusive every time we showed up at a family get-together at short notice with a new child.
It makes a huge difference and helps the child feel acknowledged and accepted.

How many kids have been in your care over the years?

In our twenty-two years of fostering, we had almost seventy kids come through our home. Their stay was anything from a single night, to a few weeks or months, and one stayed forever. We took in one to three children at a time.

What helped you during your fostering journey?

I'm a strong believer in lifelong learning. Every month I complete at least one or two courses on any subject that could help me understand these kids better.

I've completed a Diploma in Community Services and now teach these units to others. I've also taken over a hundred courses on trauma-informed care practices, complex trauma, FASD, ADHD, autism, attachment, life-story work, bullying, cyber safety, eating disorders, emotional regulation, sexualised behaviour and mental health, as well as others.

What is your big WHY?

There are twenty-six-million inhabitants of Australia, with eight million in NSW, and yet we can't seem to find homes for these kids (figures vary between 350-600 homes at any given time).

Why???? It *must* be possible.

There have to be people who would like to fill their homes with children who just want to be loved and cared for. Perhaps couples or singles who've tried IVF and decided to discontinue it.

I'd love to work closely with IVF clinics in order to give people hope. We've been through IVF as well, and I know what it entails. If they're open minded, flexible and have some patience, they could have children who stay with them permanently. Not all of them can be reunited with their birth family. It's up to the judge who presides over these cases.

When you foster, you learn a lot about how the system works, both the good and the bad, so you can make an informed decision if adoption is for you. It's important to note that all adoptions in Australia are 'open adoptions', meaning you *will* most likely continue to have contact with the birth family, the frequency of which is determined and ordered by the court.

Fostering will show you how important contact visits are for a child, so they can stay connected to their culture, have a clear identity and understand their medical history. Contact may involve the birth parents and grandparents, as well as extended family. It could even include siblings, who may also be in foster care with other families.

It's also possible that the child you're caring for has a sibling who's later added to your family. It's not uncommon to have large sibling groups of eight to eleven who are available.

Additionally, it will highlight how fostering provides you with a support system that consists of speech therapists, occupational therapists and counsellors. You'll discover how to navigate it all.

You're not alone in this. There's a team to support you, as well as a 24-hour hotline.

It's possible to receive free training through every agency. Many sessions are also available online for you to complete at your own pace. Some face to face sessions have childcare available too.

What are you passionate about?

Connecting more families with kids in need of a safe home.

We never used to have problems finding places for children under the age of five.
Now we do.

There are many sibling groups, and it breaks my heart.

What's the best thing that has ever happened to you, and why?

Three things come to my mind right away:

1. **Constantly moving**

    Moving every few years broadened my horizons. It's made me comfortable with, and appreciative of, other cultures, languages and ways of life. I'm so grateful for these opportunities that were given to me by my parents.

2. **Meeting my soul mate, David**

   David has allowed me to work when and where I wanted. He didn't always understand the bigger picture or purpose of my actions, but he still supported me. I'm eternally grateful for how he started the fostering/adoptive journey with me after being a bit apprehensive at first, as I've found most men can be.

3. **Being a parent to our three children**

   Our children are from three different sets of parents, and I love them dearly. It was never an issue for David or me if the kids looked like us or where they came from.

All three of them are precious to us in the same way, and my family means the world to me.

How did you come up with your idea of helping those who want to foster/adopt?

After hearing about the increase in the number of children in Australia, as well as those as young as two years old being 'temporarily' housed in motel rooms, I knew I had to take action!

I tried to figure out how to best put my years of experience, passion and knowledge to good use and help impact this crisis. I wanted to bridge the gap or create a powerful link and opportunity for those who

- know they want to provide a loving environment for a child/children
- don't know where to start
- want to talk to other carers to get a better understanding as to what's involved.

My vision and deep desire was to create a system whereby *each* child is able to be placed into a safe and caring home in the shortest amount of time possible. I know this may seem like an impossible task, but I needed to start somewhere.

As a result, I created a four-week program with ninety minutes each week via zoom or over the phone, to inspire and recruit new foster carers. The program is as follows:

Week One:
I help you understand

- if fostering is for you as a couple, single or LGBTQ+ community member
- how kids end up in the out-of-home care system (OOHC) in the first place
- which type of care is best for you and your current lifestyle
- the true fostering statistics
- the different agencies available in Australia
- a few agency options to choose from in your area.

Week Two:
Now it's time to move on to more pressing matters, such as

- what agencies are looking for in general
- why contact visits with the birth family are so important
- the available age group of kids in care
- case scenarios with foster kids
- how to prepare for assessor home visits.

Week Three:
To guide you through the process, I will help you understand

- the difference between fostering/adoption and guardianship
- how to start your fostering/adoption journey
- the advantages of taking on sibling groups
- possible behavioural issues.

Week Four:
Once you have decided to go on the fostering/adoption journey, we will discuss

- how to prepare your home for the big arrival
- how your extended family might be affected
- how your own family dynamics may change after a placement
- how to prepare your kids for the arrival of a foster child
- how to anticipate other issues.

I would like to help potential foster carers navigate the process of being authorised by an agency. My program educates and informs people from all walks of life, professions and cultural backgrounds.

How did you come up with the idea for your business?

It all started with the urge to write down my rather unusual life story. When my dad died, I realised I still had so many questions about his life and decided to write my life story for our three kids. In day-to-day life, we often don't share details about 'the olden age', as our daughter Madison puts it.

I also understood that in order to get more people into fostering, we needed to think outside the box, so I went on a mission to get more people interested in fostering. I intend to do that through the promotion of the book I'm currently working on, which will be completed shortly.

I also believe that carers need to be supported better when they're starting out. I don't want them to give up if and when the going gets tough.

There are so many fostering agencies to choose from, that it can be rather overwhelming. Potential carers may feel more at ease asking another carer, instead of the agency itself. They want to be able to ask 'silly' questions without worrying about not getting approved.

I want more carers, and I'm willing to spend my days supporting them.

They need a listening ear when they're frustrated or hurt by something their caseworker or foster child did or said. It's important for them to have a bouncing board for ideas on how to manage challenging behaviours when they arise and someone to guide them to where they may find help and support.

I'm honoured to go on the fostering journey with them, so they stay on track and don't give up.

What benefits does your business offer?

Guidance
My goal is to guide you through

- the fostering maze
- finding the right agency that fits your needs/wants & suggesting 2-3 agencies in your area
- what happens during the assessment process.

Expertise
Based on my over twenty years of experience and as an adoptive mum, I provide you with

- expert data and knowledge about fostering/adoption/guardianship in Australia
- case studies that detail 'what if' scenarios as compared to typical ones
- tips on how to prepare the child and yourself for contact visits with birth families

- tips based on information acquired during Shared Lives and Open Adoption courses
- trauma-informed care principles and basic neuroscience in regard to trauma.

Assurance
As an internationally certified coach, I will coach you in regard to

- any initial doubts or concerns you may have
- how your own belief and value system may influence your fostering/adoption journey
- preparing your own children for the arrival of a foster kid (if applicable)
- figuring out the right time to come onboard.

Readiness
Once you've made your decision, I offer support by

- helping you get into the right mindset before a placement
- getting your home ready for a child's arrival
- preparing the foster child's room
- knowing what to ask before the child is brought into your home
- providing tips on how to prepare your extended family
- guiding you in regard to any concerns you may have about possible changes to your family dynamics.

GEAR UP, and let's do this!

Contact me for a free discovery call to figure out if fostering is for you and if we're a good fit.

If you're caring already, I'm happy to provide you with ongoing support to talk things through, and as a coach, I'm happy to support you, so all areas of your life are aligned.

Who is this program for?

This program is for anyone who's ever

- thought about becoming a carer
- wondered if they would actually meet the criteria
- tried to fall pregnant and it hasn't happened yet
- gone through unsuccessful IVF cycles
- wanted a sibling for their child
- been overwhelmed by too many agency choices
- been disheartened when an agency didn't call them back after an enquiry
- considered adoption/guardianship
- become an empty nester and misses having children in their home
- been interested in the A-Z of fostering.

Why do you think there aren't enough homes for kids in need within Australia?

There are several reasons, in my opinion:

- **Not advertising in the right places**

    Though heaps of money is spent on advertising, I don't feel it's being explained enough or marketed to the right candidates. Why are we not holding talks in schools, places of worship or with other community service providers? Why are we not targeting IVF Clinics? Why do we not have more interviews with real carers sharing their experiences? Why do we seem to always show the negative stories of kids in foster care? We could maybe even have birth families share experiences, where they appreciated the carers taking over while they got their lives back on track.

    We should all work together even more, improve our support systems and have an increased amount of respect for one another.

- **Myths**

    Some of the myths in regard to fostering in general include having to be married, ceasing work for a year or not being approved if you belong to the LGBTQ+ community, all of which are untrue.

- **Apprehension**

    You may be apprehensive about getting started if you've had a life with many lows. You might be afraid that people will judge you about your past. Depending on what you've gone through, it's often these very life experiences that will help you connect with those in need, as you've gone through it and come out the other side.

- ❖ **People thinking they're not eligible, because of their busy lifestyle**

    There are those who seem to think there needs to be a 'perfect time' to get started with fostering. You might be doing shift work right now. You know what? That's life, and childcare can be arranged through your support system. But it still means that this child, who may have been rather unsupervised in the past, now has a safe and loving place to come home to.

- ❖ **Confusion**

    NSW alone has over fifty agencies to choose from, and many people don't know where to start. They're overwhelmed by so many choices. But once they understand that each agency often specialises in certain services, it becomes much clearer. For example, some agencies specialise in placing kids with a disability, while others place those who come up for adoption or locate homes for teenagers.

- ❖ **Not enough information**

    Did you know that you don't have to be married to foster a child? Or that many children are fostered into loving LGBTQ+ households? Did you know that you can live in a rental property or that you could take foster kids on holidays? Did you know that you receive a tax-free fortnightly payment, so it doesn't become a huge financial burden for you?

    So many people think they have to be living a perfect life with two parents and a white picket fence, but it isn't true, because that's just *not* real life.

What if someone can't foster full-time, but they still want to help?

If you can't foster full-time, there are many other options.

Emergency Care

Emergency Care is often provided by the Department of Community and Justice (DCJ, formerly known as FACS/DOCS), as it involves the immediate removal of children. They might be removed on a Friday night when offices are closed, and it takes a bit of time to find relatives or a foster family who can take them in.

Respite Care

This is when you get a beginning and an end date, where you help out foster families on regular weekends or with one-off placements, such as filling in for the carer if they need to be away for a period of time, like for a hospital stay or to look after an elderly parent.

Restoration Care

This can last for up to two years before the kids are placed back with their birth families.

Permanent Care

Permanent care provides help for kids, until they reach the age of eighteen. Obviously, once you've been fostering a child for many years, you don't have to say goodbye to them if you don't want to. It really depends on the relationship you've developed.

How do you know if you've made a difference through fostering?

These are some of the tell-tale signs you've made a difference in their lives:

- They start taking pride in their appearance.

- They realise it's not their fault that they're in care and understand they didn't break up their parents' relationship.
- They start believing they're beautiful, inside and out.
- They want to do well in school, because they realise someone cares if they do.
- They lean in as you're reading a book to them, when at first they sat far away.
- They take your hand while crossing the road and won't let go.
- They learn to name their emotions and are able to control them.
- They insist that *you* have to tuck them in at night.
- They start making plans for the future.
- They feel proud of their achievements.
- They disclose the abuse to you, because they trust you.
- They say, "I love you", and they really, really mean it.
- They smile and laugh, because they feel safe.
- They can sleep without nightmares.
- They no longer hide food 'just in case' they'll feel hungry.

Who else would you like to work with?

Anyone who would like to hear what a foster carer has to say. For instance, I would like to speak with school principals and their staff who want to make a difference in a foster child's life, as well as birth families that are open to learn and not judge carers too quickly. This also works the other way around, of course. There are carers who aren't as non-judgemental of birth families as they could be.

I'm willing to talk to caseworkers who wonder how little ones settle when they drop them off at a carer's home in the middle of the night (for emergency care only), and also give tips on how they may be able to connect better with carers.

In addition, I'm willing to do mediation between caseworkers, foster carers and birth families. We all have our struggles, and we should work together more closely to support a child who's stuck in the middle.

What's the biggest tip you could give new carers?

Ask for help.

It seems obvious, but many carers feel that if they admit they're struggling, caseworkers may think poorly of them. Or in a worst-case scenario, that the kids might be taken away. When a carer is struggling, it doesn't necessarily mean the kid needs to leave that home, that they're unloved or that bonding hasn't taken place yet.

It just means that at this point in time, the behaviour is tough to manage or understand.

What's the best way to support potential foster carers who are just getting started?

I would tell them to book in for a free call on my website, and we'll have a twenty-minute chat to see if fostering could be for them. Upfront, I can say they'd need a spare bedroom, but most other issues can often be sorted.

If you're someone who's considered fostering, I'd love to go on that journey with you. I'll give you my honest opinion, and there are packages I offer for ongoing support to help carers in these areas.

Do you have an inspiring carer story?

During a doctor visit, our foster child was playing with another little girl who didn't want to share. Her mother told me that she would have loved having another kid who could help her child learn these skills. I told her about fostering and where to start, and invited her and her husband to our place for coffee. Six months later, they were the proud carers of two more kids.

What about those who regularly deal with kids who've suffered trauma?

In my opinion, any parent or carer of kids who's had significant events happen in their lives, even something as common as divorce, should look into trauma-informed care practice courses offered by the Australian Childhood Foundation or equivalent. These are vital not only for caseworkers, but for *everyone*.

There are teachers who tend to punish a child for stealing food, rather than understanding that their underlying fear of going hungry is the overriding force, or they may be exhibiting attention-seeking behaviour as a way of saying they're attention-needing.

Kids often think they're the cause of rifts with their parents, even though it may have to do with intergenerational trauma and the way their parents were parented.

It's important to learn about neuroscience and its plasticity. Our brain can repair itself, although slowly, through consistency, patience and repetition.

I'm keen to share the knowledge and resources I've gained over the years. If I'd known then what I know now, I would have understood the reasoning behind a child's actions much better and would have reacted differently in a few scenarios.

Sometimes it can be hard for busy carers to take the time to fully understand what's going on, when they just want to do what they've always done. But children with a trauma background need slightly different ways of parenting, as we don't know all of their history.

Every child is different, yet certain behaviours repeat themselves.

What is a common issue for these kids coming into care?

Emotional regulation is a common one.

They've often spent their whole lives in fight-flight-freeze scenarios, which are the survival skills that helped them cope with everyday challenges.

When a child has a tantrum, the carer may not yet know what triggered it, but by naming the emotion through saying, "I can see that you're angry right now", kids start to understand the emotion, and then you can 'tame it' by putting strategies in place regarding what to do next time they're 'angry'. They might learn to punch pillows, do breathing exercises and/or remove themselves from the scene, so they no longer hit other kids when they feel like this again.

How does life change for a kid who's forced to enter the out-of-home care system?

They lose everything they've known so far in their lives. There's the loss of family, teachers, friends, sport coaches, pets and all of their material comforts (if any).

They often have a shame-based identity of, "There must be something wrong with me. I must be a bad kid".

The number of bad experiences within the first eighteen years, particularly the first three of those years, have a huge effect on physical and mental issues later.

What do these kids need the most?

Routine, safety, predictability and patience.

They need to learn to trust and build relationships that are reciprocal. It's important for them to understand that if an adult promises something, it will be done, and that grownups can be relied upon. It's the emotional relationship template for their entire future.

They need a secure environment where they can form their identity and learn to self-regulate their emotions.

Just *one* reliable, secure attachment can show them that they're lovable and worthy of our time. Then they can start to create beliefs about themselves that are positive while developing empathy and compassion for others, thus becoming more resilient in life.

What if it's not a good match?

When you take in a child, and it's really not working well for you, or maybe they don't get along with your partner or your biological child, then you need to bring up the concern with your caseworker as soon as possible. Sometimes it's little things that are upsetting your child, and you don't know about it.

When our biological child was three. he really struggled with the foster child calling me 'mum' from the moment he walked through our door. There was competition and jealousy. Once I explained to my son that the child had been with many carers, and that anyone who looked after him would be called *mum* no matter the timeframe, he started to understand. It took a while, but we got the foster child to call me 'aunty', and I included my boy in the teaching process.

Another issue came up when the foster children would use cuss words, and our kids didn't understand why they couldn't use them. We asked our children to help us teach our house rules and to find words they could use instead.

If it's a bigger issue from either side, discuss it with your agency.

It's not easy for anyone involved, but *your* family will always have to come first. There's no other way. If you're not a happy, well-functioning home, you can't accept another child into it.

What do you think is the hardest part of fostering?

Letting go.

Yes, it's a big one, and it doesn't necessarily get easier with the years. But it also means that fostering was a success for this particular child. The overall aim is to reunite them with their birth family after they've made significant life changes that justify to the court it's safe for the child to be returned.

Is it always the correct decision? No, as the system definitely isn't perfect. But we're here to help out, not to act as a judge. As carers, we never know the full story from all sides involved. We're emotionally involved, and the judge is not, so they look at the overall picture and decide each child's future.

What does 'open adoption' mean for a family?

The court decides how often you will need to meet with the birth family, or any significant others like siblings, etc. On average, these meetings may be scheduled two to four times a year. This isn't easy for all adoptive parents, as it can be a rather complex issue, but the more it does work, the more connected the adopted child feels to their culture and identity. Questions about their medical history can also be answered, and it helps solidify an understanding of their past.

If it's harmonious, there are an extra few people you can add to your extended family.

How does your story relate to elevating someone's performance?

If through my work I can elevate a carer's self-esteem and make them feel happier about the selfless work they do, then that automatically elevates their performance.

If any kinship carer feels heard and more supported, it will elevate their daily performance in looking after a child, as visits with their relatives may be rather complex.

If an adoptive parent feels supported, and therefore doesn't give up during the draining adoption process, it will make them a better parent who doesn't even think twice about giving a child a permanent place to live.

I want to give hope to anyone who wants to fill their home with the pitter-patter of tiny feet, so it may elevate them and help them feel complete as a family.

What is your vision for a better future?

My hope is that birth families are even better supported, so kids don't end up in the foster care system to start with.

What is the one message you wish to share with the world?

That there's never a 'right time' to have kids. There are always possible excuses to delay looking into fostering, or even adoption. Initially, I struggled to combine the two. I never wanted people to come into fostering, because they wanted to create or increase their family.

As of 2020, there are 47,000 children in care in Australia, with 17,000 in out-of-home care (OOHC) in NSW alone, which means there are plenty of kids who need permanent homes.

My advice would be to get dual authorisation, which means getting authorised for fostering and adoption at the same time, if that's what you'd like to do.

Some agencies do offer both, but I would suggest *always* beginning with fostering, in order to understand what it entails.

Fostering means being open to contact with birth families, going to many doctor appointments for check-ups, working within a team setting and educating yourself about trauma-informed care practices. With each child in your care, you learn and grow as a carer of kids 'who aren't born under your heart, but in it'.

The chances are rather great that a kid won't just stay for one night or even several weeks. They can stay for up to two years in 'restoration care', as this is the timeframe given to birth families for them to demonstrate significant changes in their lifestyle, before the court decides if they will move into 'permanent or long-term care', meaning that they remain a ward of the state until the age of eighteen.

Adoptions from OOHC are now being approved quicker than ever, as research has shown that kids thrive with boundaries and consistency, rather than being moved from home to home. Some have had up to twenty placements by the age of eighteen.

Once they've been in the OOHC system for more than two years, they're eligible for either guardianship (used mostly by Torres Straight Islanders/Aboriginal Peoples and kids in kinship care) or adoption.

How can the readers of this book help your mission?

- ▸ Spread the word, so every safe home that wants a child, gets one.
- ▸ Plant a seed when you hear someone say they would like a child in their life.

- Don't overthink things. Just get started.

- Book in for a chat on my website or connect through LinkedIn, so we can start the conversation, and I can help you make an informed decision.

Kids are getting removed from homes all over Australia, *every single night*, and we don't have enough foster homes available to provide them with a safe family setting.

Let's change this together!

 To discover more about how Irina can help you *Elevate Your Performance*, simply visit

www.elevatebooks.com/performance

Jase Dreger
Futureproof

Jase Dreger is a highly effective personal transformation and retirement coach, speaker and author, with over twenty years of finance experience.

He's worked with some of the largest organisations in Australia to help improve their employees' financial literacy, decrease their financial stress and improve their well-being by delivering programs that aim to educate and empower at every life stage of life, right through to retirement.

Jase combines his experience as a myotherapist and holistic health practitioner to create his FutureProof360 method, the motto of which is 'live well, work well, retire well'.

Jase has a passion for positive ageing, and his personal life experiences as a carer have led him to become an advocate for effective mental health management at all ages.

Jase Dreger

Futureproof

How do you start your day?

I wake up and thank God I'm alive.

Jokes aside, my day starts with me walking into another room to turn off the alarm clock, because I'm not naturally a morning person. However, I wanted to be a morning person, and this little trick helps. Then I set my intention for the day, say some positive affirmations, get some form of exercise and prepare my kids for school.

How do these strategies make a difference to your success?

I'm on a quest to be the healthiest and fittest I've ever been. I'm a life-long learner, widely read. I do the work. I've enrolled in the PHD program at Authentic Education, and I'm trying to say yes more than no, while doing what I can to get out of my own way.

What are your favourite ways to relax and enjoy life?

Spending time with my family and friends. I also love being active, especially anything having to do with the water, such as boating, fishing, swimming, and paddle boarding. I also love hiking and mountain biking, as well as exercising my creative side with woodworking and landscaping.

How do you stay inspired on a daily basis?

Healing myself, so I can help others heal themselves and overcome their challenges in life.

Also, being the best role model I can be for my boys, family and friends, and making a difference in people's lives.

The urge to learn as much as I can in order to help others inspires me. By the time people reach retirement, they've had major negative moments, so I can help them by passing on my knowledge. I'd like to think that my own struggles meant something, and some good can come out of each negative experience.

Sometimes people become bitter and angry at the world, which consciously or subconsciously carries into their retirement. They now have more unstructured time on their hands, so if these issues aren't resolved, it can lead to an unhappy retirement, full of resentment and unhappiness.

Sometimes the symptoms can be more subtle, like weariness or a sense of trepidation and fear about what life might throw at them. Entering retirement with some apprehension is normal and even healthy, but it's important to recognise if it's an indicator of some greater anxiety, because being in fear can result in an unfulfilled life in retirement.

Uncovering these obstacles during coaching sessions inspires me, because I know that by addressing them head on, I can help people leave those negative experiences behind and even find meaning in them, which sets them up for a truly rewarding retirement.

What is the main thing that gives your life meaning?

My past experiences haven't always been smooth sailing. This has created deep pain, emotionally and psychologically, and has robbed me of a large part of my life.

For a long period of time, there wasn't a single day I allowed myself to be happy. As soon as I started laughing or enjoying myself, I'd stop.

I never gave myself permission to be authentic, because I was forever looking back with what I call the trifecta of regret, guilt and shame, constantly living with emotional pain and a longing to be free from it. Helping others break free allows me to be my authentic self.

The realisation that past experiences were valuable, developed a burning desire and curiosity to understand people on a much deeper level. This quest to understand myself has led me to uncover how and why we're all connected, which in turn propelled me to remain open to looking at life through my own lens. I want my life to mean something and to halt the pain cycle by sharing my journey with my family in ways I didn't experience growing up.

I feel empowered knowing I can inspire others to realise their own superpowers.

What are your biggest life lessons?

There are many. It's almost like choosing your favourite child. These are the three that come to mind:

- **The duality of life**

    Sometimes in the search for happiness, you can unconsciously embrace unhappiness, which then lengthens the duration and depth of unsatisfied feelings.

- **The power of gratitude, love and appreciation**

    I can still recall the time I fully learned the meaning and importance of gratitude. It was when I first started practising meditation, which was like opening a door to vast amounts of knowledge, appreciation and awakening. Before I started regularly meditating, life kept throwing me into one crisis after another, and I was angry at not only the injustice of it all, but also the toll it was taking on me and my loved ones.

Anger is usually a sign that you're frustrated about something or someone and may feel powerless, not validated or unfairly treated. If ignored over a period of time, it can have a cumulative effect that impacts your ability to cope with even the smallest life stressors.

Through regular meditative practice, I discovered the importance of gratitude. This taught me to focus on all the things I did have in my life and not on what was lacking. The best antidote for anger is gratitude. Try being angry and grateful at the same time.

As the anger subsided, and my appreciation for my life grew, I was able to be open to receiving and giving love. And probably the most important of all, I started on a pathway of self-love.

This has not come easily for me. As is often the case with anger, it has many friends such as shame, guilt, regret and pain. I feel incredibly blessed to have unlocked the door. It's allowed me to go on a journey of acceptance of myself, and everything and everyone around me. The colours are brighter, the days are fuller, the sounds are richer, and life becomes beautiful both in its appearance and meaning. Allowing myself to overcome long-held limiting beliefs and perceptions has opened a gateway of vast knowledge and wisdom. And though I may be at the beginning of my journey, it's led me to the realisation that I wanted to help others.

- ❖ **Determining your highest values**

    It's important to determine your values and the pivotal role they play in governing all that you are. Many of us follow values instilled in us by parents, teachers or society that may not represent our true selves. Being aligned with your highest values leaves you feeling fulfilled and happy, while being misaligned with them leaves you unfulfilled and unhappy.

Your highest values are a bit like your name. You carry them with you wherever you go. They're central to your identity and understanding who you are and who you aspire to be.

Identifying your highest values can often have a huge transformational impact. You learn who you are, and who you've always been, for the very first time.

Learning your highest values can reassure you that you're living an authentic life. It reduces self-doubt, propelling you forward with clarity, purpose and meaning.

What does love mean to you?

Love means everything. I first learned about love through loss and grief. I can't say that I've attended any more funerals than anyone else I know, but each of them had a profound impact on me. Whether it was a family member's funeral, or one for a friend or work colleague, I can distinctively remember being overcome with heavy emotions, unanswered questions, and a greater appreciation for the fragility of life and the legacy we all want to leave.

Later in life, I came to fully appreciate love through marriage to my wife and the birth of our two boys. I learned that there are different types and depths of love. There's unconditional love, like what you have for your child and the kind shared through friendship and common bonds. But I also learned that self-love is important, because you can't love others if you don't love yourself first. Sometimes it can be hard to do, and its importance can be neglected or overlooked.

I know that people think it's easier to care for others. They might even believe they're being selfish thinking about their own needs, so they put the health and happiness of others first. But this only leads to poor health and a lack of vitality. It's like when you're on a plane, and they tell you to put the oxygen mask on yourself before you attend to your child.

If you were speaking to your younger self, what advice would you give?

If you love what you do, and you can find a way to help others, you're on the right path.

The journey of life ebbs and flows like ocean waves.

Don't just follow the crowd. Be an individual, independent and self-driven.

Remember to play and look for the fun in everything you do.

Determine your highest values, and allow them to guide you in whatever you do.

Listen to your intuition, and make time to listen to others with the goal of understanding them, not responding to them.

Time is precious. Learn to value it. Don't put off until tomorrow what you can do today.

Pay attention to what you eat and drink. Hydration is key. Eat foods that make you feel energised and lift your spirits. What you consume can have an impact on your mood. It's not just a matter of having a balanced diet or eating in moderation. Make your choices from the food groups that are best for you, and find a good naturopath.

Exercise. There's power in movement. Always remember to stretch and meditate. Also, learn how to breathe properly for the full calming effects.

Creativity and imagination are nourishment for the soul. Create not only with your mind but also your heart, and you'll move the impossible to the possible.

Be kind to yourself, so you can be open to having meaningful and loving connections with others.

Embrace all facets of being human, the good, the bad and the ugly.

There are fifty-three senses. Know what they are and the importance and power of all of them.

Be curious. Live and think like an adventurer or explorer. Never lose the joy and wonder you had as a small child.

Knowledge can be acquired not only in the classroom, but through the school of life. Learn something new daily, and remember it like you will one day have to teach it.

Learn about the twenty-seven basic emotions and how to regulate them.

You will play many roles in your life. It's where your relationships exist. Invest time in all of them, whether it's with family, or as a friend or mentor.

Progress or improvement is made through consistently taking small actions that are aligned with your highest values. The choices you make and don't make will directly determine who you are and where you are at any given moment.

Tomorrow will take care of itself if you look after yourself today.

If you're unsure of something, don't forget to ask for help. Be open to other people's view of the world, their opinions and perceptions. There are many pearls of wisdom that can come from those who are older and/or have more life experience. Life is not a dress rehearsal. Don't wait for the time to be right, or it may just pass you by.

Remember to have balance. When planning your day, make sure you prioritise sleep, meditation, and reflection. It's the only way you'll have the energy to get everything done. Don't try and take on too much.

Spend as much time as you can in nature. Use your senses to take in all the sights, sounds and smells of the outdoors. Learn to appreciate the power of silence.

How would you like to be remembered?

As a great father, husband, friend, son, and all-round good human.

As someone who made a difference in the lives of others as a healer, teacher, mentor, advisor and confidante.

As someone who said yes to life, who was loyal, always saw the best in others and helped others see the best in themselves.

What would you like your legacy to be?

I want my legacy to be that I helped people realise their potential. I would like to know that I touched the lives of everyone I came in contact with, and that they were able to experience life's joy and magic, as well as a deep love and appreciation of life.

I would hope that I healed people by helping them identify their own unique values and working together to navigate their life transitions.

I'd like to know that I instilled a sense of self-worth and security in my sons, so when they're out in the world, they feel confident enough to take risks, try new things and chase their dreams, while making a positive difference in the lives of others and the world around them.

I would also hope I was a great role model and a beacon of hope for others.

Jase Dreger

Have you had any aha moments that changed everything for you?

There are many aha moments, but for me it was when I learned to take responsibility for myself. For as long as I can remember, I was angry and frustrated with myself. I knew I wanted better and that I was capable of more.

My aha moment came around the age of sixteen. I felt weighed down by the expectations of my family, my school, society in general and my coaches. My whole life was already mapped out, and I wasn't at all sure it was the life I wanted. I'd always done what was expected of me.

Then one day it dawned on me that I had the power to change my life. I had choices. I could make my own decisions and create my own future version of myself.

It started with modifying my diet and starting an exercise routine. This was in an era where few people worried about such things, but I became fascinated by the ways diet and exercise affected the brain and body. As I saw my body transform into something I didn't think was possible for me, I also felt the transformation in my mind and how that affected my sense of self. It morphed into reading everything I could about personal development and set me on a pathway of self-discovery and self-improvement.

What's the best thing that's ever happened to you, and why?

Marrying my beautiful wife, of course! She makes me want to be a better person, and we created two beautiful boys who make it all worthwhile. Building a family of my own gave me a new vigour, a new start. It was the greatest motivator to live a life I was proud of.

What is your big WHY?

To help people navigate their transition through life's challenges, so they can realise their unique superpowers and connect to their authentic self.

What do you believe you've been put on the planet to do, and how are you making a difference in people's lives?

I help people appreciate that they're enough and have always been. This aids them in connecting their future self to who they are today, so they can reframe their self-limiting beliefs to live a life of purpose, meaning and fulfillment, and understand they matter and deserve it.

Throughout my career, I've spoken to thousands of workers as they approach retirement. Most are well aware of the importance of being financially prepared. Some plan many years in advance, determined to save as much money as possible for their retirement, while others do so when only a few years from retirement age, content with relying on the government's aged pension.

But this is generally the only plan people make, while neglecting to consider any other aspect of their retirement. They may have some vague ideas of going on an overseas holiday or spending more time on the golf course, but nothing further than that.

One year into retirement, these people report dissatisfaction in their personal relationships, depression, boredom, disconnection with society, physical health problems and a lack of purpose.

I want to prevent this from happening, so I work with clients before their retirement. I take them through a series of questions to identify their values and develop a unique comprehensive plan that incorporates all areas of life, not just financial, to set them up for a successful retirement.

What's the difference between happiness and fulfillment?

Happiness and fulfillment are similar but different. For me, happiness is a joyous moment in time that passes. It's like seeing your favourite sporting team win or having a laugh with friends.

While fulfillment may not feel as intense as happiness does, it's longer-lasting and tends to come after a length of time and/or concerted effort.

In the same way, retirement today differs from the historical definition that our parents and grandparents modelled their own retirement on.

It's about a new beginning and an opportunity, maybe for the very first time, to live according to your highest values.

What are you passionate about?

I'm passionate about coaching, teaching, role modelling, mentoring people through life-stage transitions and retirement well-being.

Why did you start your retirement coaching business?

My reason for starting my retirement coaching business was to ensure people are adequately prepared for their retirement. I want to develop a plan for all my clients that has them living a satisfying and fulfilling retirement life. Of course, financial security plays a role in that, but so does physical and mental health.

One of the ways to find your joy, is to identify your values. When you live a life that's aligned with your values, a fulfilling life comes rather easily. If you base it on the expectations of others or what you think is right due to what society tells you, then a dissonance occurs that can lead to frustration and dissatisfaction.

How do you help your clients identify their values?

Typically, it takes a number of coaching sessions. Often we discover they're not living completely by their own values or that their retirement plans are actually at odds with their values.

Coaching involves listening to their life story and taking them through a process of self-discovery to identify their highest values. We do this through extensive questionnaires, finding out what they naturally gravitate towards doing, what gets them thinking, what their feelings are around family and what they've always wanted to do but never had the opportunity or courage to.

FutureProof 360 is a multi-disciplinary approach that educates and inspires people to connect with the future version of themselves at each life stage. It's s a proven methodology that helps remove the barriers limiting them from being all that they can be, so they can retire on their own terms and reinforces our company motto: 'Live well, work well, retire well'.

These are the steps we take our clients through to uncover those parts of themselves that light them up and give them joy, so they're able to identify who they truly are and have always been:

1. I ask them to envision or imagine themselves out into the future, using all of their senses to tell me what they see, hear, smell, feel and taste.

2. We look at current behaviours, habits and actions, and whether they're aligned with the future vision or expectations they have of themselves.

3. We examine what's been holding them back or getting in the way of achieving their dream life.

4. Through a proven methodology, we nurture them through a process to dissolve that part of them that's no longer serving them.

5. We offer them the option to reset and align their actions with their future vision.

How did you become interested in retirement well-being?

Personally, I became interested after watching my parents and grandparents work hard and save, sacrificing or delaying gratification for a later point in time.

Professionally, I started to see the same pattern. It became apparent that whether you were fully or partially self-funded financially in retirement, it didn't guarantee you were happy or prepared adequately for life in retirement.

I witnessed firsthand, both personally and professionally, people transitioning into retirement who were already burned out, so rather than being excited about retirement, they were overwhelmed by the reality of it.

Preparing for a mentally healthy retirement is just as important as preparing financially.

People entering retirement today, often tell me they're just getting started. They don't feel old, and the last thing they want is to be seen or treated as such.

I'm also a strong advocate for positive ageing. As a society, we have a long way to go to truly embracing it, particularly in the workforce, where it could be seen as an asset.

With ageing comes wisdom through experience. It's well-documented that the ageing population globally is a mega-trend that will have an economic impact equal to, if not greater than, the magnitude of technology.

People can have an identity crisis post work, as they've defined who they are according to their name and occupation. In retirement, they face the reality that they no longer have an identity. It often leaves them feeling unfulfilled.

What courses have you taken that enabled you to get started or build your business?

- Certified retirement coaching courses
- Applied Science Myotherapy
- Advance dip financial planning, including superannuation, wealth creation and financial well-being
- Bachelor of Business in Financial Planning
- Various holistic courses, including mental health, nutrition, functional fitness, strength and conditioning, gerontology, positive ageing and Psychometry
- Authentic Education's PHD Program
- Authentic Education Platinum Partner
- Dr John Demartini: Breakthrough Experience
- Brandon Bays: The Journey intensive program

How do you go from a concept or idea to a business?

❖ Do market research to identify if there's a need for your idea. An important question to keep in mind is if there's a problem that needs solving, and if you have a solution that can help.

- ❖ Identify a good coach or mentor to help you bring your idea or dream to life. Ideally, it should be someone who has a proven track record in achieving success for others, so you can use their blueprint.

- ❖ Develop an action-orientated plan that details small tasks and key milestones.

- ❖ Follow a proven methodology that gets results in the shortest possible time.

- ❖ Ask the right questions, and once you've implemented your plan, have the courage to consistently take action. Make decisions quickly without having to get it right.

- ❖ Acquire the right knowledge and skills. Believe in yourself, work hard, and surround yourself with people who are prepared to invest in you and your vision just as much as you are. Find like-minded groups, where you can test and share your ideas.

- ❖ Be prepared to listen to others, be flexible in your thinking and always remain open to new perspectives.

- ❖ Find complimentary partners and companies that can elevate you, so you can both add more value to the very people you're serving.

What's the biggest mistake people make in the area of retirement planning?

Planning for retirement as though it's only a financial event. It's not. It's a life stage transition. By seeing it only in terms of dollars and cents, they're severely limiting their options.

People often overlook how they've been doing largely the same thing for decades. Going to work creates structure in people's lives, and the job they do creates their identity.

Work provides us with meaning and purpose. If we remove the purpose of getting up in the morning and being somewhere at a certain time, for a set length of time, we often feel a sense of disorientation.

Historically, retirement was seen as the time you stopped working and began playing golf, travelling or seeing out your final days in a quiet retirement village. But while these may be on your bucket list, after the post-work honeymoon period is over, you'll be left saying, "I need more".

The contemporary definition of retirement is about a new beginning. A period of reflection and following long-held life dreams. You may look to study, give back, or take up hobbies or interests that foster connection and adventure. Or look to volunteering your time locally, on community projects or with sporting clubs. You may even find a part-time job in a local hardware store or coffee shop, take up teaching or help those who are less fortunate.

Retirement can be bad for your health, as well as highly disruptive to your social and friendship network, creating a sense of isolation and loneliness. If you've been working for many years at a job that involved highly skilled, intensive labour, stopping abruptly can have a serious effect on your well-being.

A silent epidemic facing older people is alcohol and substance abuse. Without the need to be somewhere the next day, that late-afternoon time period, which would normally be beer or wine o'clock on the weekend, often becomes a daily practice.

And then there are couples who reintroduce themselves to each other after many years of marriage. There's a big difference in retirement planning where one half of a couple wants to retire, while the other is happy to continue working. This is particularly the case if there's an age gap.

A single male going into retirement who identifies himself through his work has a different transition from a woman who has recently separated from her husband.

Some women fall into a caretaking role, looking out for young children or an elderly parent, and are therefore financially vulnerable. This means they may have had significant periods of time outside of paid employment, which limits their superannuation and general savings, but perhaps ignites a passion to pursue a long-held goal once their caretaking role has finished.

What's the best tip you could give these people?

Look at retirement planning through the lens of health and well-being, not your account balance.

What do you think people's biggest problems in life are?

That's a big question that requires a multi-faceted answer. I'm always cautious about oversimplifying challenges faced by a few and correlating them to those shared by everyone. I'm also conscious that what may be perceived as an issue for one group of people, may very well be the envy of another, particularly if we're taking a global view.

People are preconditioned to live according to society's expectations about how they should define happiness, which is usually incongruent with their highest values.

They often measure their degree of retirement happiness on their financial capacity to afford their desired lifestyle. However, it's not just about being able to meet the cost of retirement in the first year, but considering the very real risk that they may outlive their money.

I want to encourage people to look beyond their financial capacity and consider their emotional and psychological well-being. After all, what's the point of improving their financial capacity if their psychological faculties are poor or being ignored? By coaching them to work out their goals, they can look forward to a well-rounded retirement.

How do you encourage people to consider their emotional and psychological well-being and not just their finances?

What I've found in my work is that people are exhausted. The rapid pace of the modern world, and the expectations we place on ourselves to perform better than yesterday, weighs heavily on the mind and body.

People understand the importance of having money in retirement, but either they don't consider other areas of their lives or think it will work itself out.

My way of encouraging them to consider their emotional and psychological capacity is to point out that many people haven't stopped to evaluate what they truly want out of life. They've done things almost on autopilot, following the well-worn path of many before them. They've done what's expected of them, which may or may not align with their own desires and aspirations.

Then when they do reach retirement, they're faced with a range of physical and psychological symptoms they can no longer ignore. But rather than prioritise their time to address the origins or root cause of their problems, they reach out for another coffee, or one more glass of wine or a beer for the road. They suppress the pain with medication or eat their way through the uncomfortable feelings.

This is why it's important to have a one-on-one consultation with a retirement coach to go over all areas of your life, identify your unique goals, remove any obstacles and develop your unique retirement plan.

How do you create this plan?

One of the tools we use to evaluate emotional and psychological capacity for retirement is the Framework of 15. These are a series of questions in fifteen different categories designed to find out

1. how much of their identity they receive from their work

2. what they plan to do with their retirement

3. if they see retirement as a loss or a gain and why

4. if they control how they spend their time or rely on someone else to decide for them

5. if they have a positive or negative attitude towards retirement

6. who they're modelling their retirement after, such as parents, friends or work colleagues

7. the dynamics of their relationships

8. if they and their spouse plan on retiring at the same time

9. what their dream retirement looks like

10. their current state of health, functional fitness, flexibility and vitality, and their attitude towards health

11. how they'll spend their time

12. their definition of leisure and what it looks like

13. how they can share their wisdom

14. if they want to continue working in retirement, and if so, what kind of work they'd like to do

15. what they'll do for fun and relaxation

16. what they'll look forward to each day

17. what they want their legacy to be

What skills and/or tools do you possess that can help clients?

I hold an advanced diploma in financial planning, and I'm a certified retirement coach, which gives me a number of tools to use during coaching sessions.

I've worked in the finance industry for over twenty-five years, and during that time I've accumulated over 200,000 conversations with people about planning for their financial future.

What I've learned is that people tend to focus solely on the financial. Their concerns are understandably centred around having enough money to retire on, how much superannuation they should be aiming for, how to build wealth and protect it, and relying on their own savings or aged pension.

These are important and valid questions, but focussing solely on the financial aspect of retirement meant they were doing themselves a disservice. This understanding led me to developing my own retirement coaching business.

Prior to entering the financial world, I was a qualified myotherapist and personal trainer, so I'm able to bring my knowledge of body mechanics, exercise and diet to my coaching business.

How do goals keep someone motivated?

Goals help keep you motivated, because they're something to aim for and look forward to. They're your highest priorities. That said, the goals you set yourself have to reflect what's most important to you. That's why I believe you need to make sure your goals reflect your true desires by discussing them with a qualified coach.

Your highest values will naturally propel you forward without it feeling like a big effort. Therefore, if the goal isn't aligned with your higher/shadow values, you likely won't reach it, or if you do, it won't meet or exceed your expectations. It's like thinking if you reach the top of a mountain, your dreams will be realised. But when you get there, it's unsatisfying, because you realise you were following someone else's idea of happiness.

When they say it's not the destination, it's the journey, it's true. If you enjoy the process, you know that the goal is in alignment with your true self. As you reach your micro goals (small goals leading up to the major one) you're satisfying your underlying (shadow) values. The choices you make, and don't make, move you towards what you most desire and away from what you least desire.

If the goal isn't aligned with your highest priorities, there will often be a lot of effort initially (physical and mentally), but it will drop off because there's a disconnect between your goal and what your authentic self wants.

People who reach a particular goal, for example weight loss, talk about how much weight they lost, while also describing the intangible benefits, such as, going off their medication and having more energy and self-confidence.

What they're really saying is that losing weight has allowed them to be seen, validated and recognised, which is their real motivation, or shadow value. It's what got them out of bed when they didn't want to, helped them say no to unhealthy snacks and above all else, remain focused and consistent, day in and day out, until they reached their goal.

Any meaningful advice on how to get through a truly difficult time?

The most meaningful advice I can offer to people during a difficult time is to continue holding on to hope. Even when all seems lost, focusing on hope gives you that crack in the door to find your way out. Trying to figure out what you can be grateful for in the midst of enormous difficulties, while visualising the future you're hoping for, isn't easy, but it's necessary in order to navigate through an intense life crisis.

I remember when my mum underwent a bone marrow transplant. I wanted to be her voice of hope and strength. I told her we weren't going to focus on the negatives but solely on the smallest of wins or moments of gratitude. Mum needed to fight this in her mind just as much as in her body. Each day I would collect the small wins and let her know she was moving in the right direction. All she had to do was rest and future focus, allowing her mind to see what she wanted to do once she got out.

Eventually, she was able to see the benefit in this approach and was able to do it on her own. In the end, she was able to heal and move forward.

What mindset do you believe you need to create a great life?

A mindset that is positive, open to possibilities and flexible in order to cope with life's adversities.

To create a positive, open and flexible mindset, you must first consider what your intentions are and who you want to be in five or ten years. Then you need to look at your current habits, your way of thinking, and your behaviours to discover if they're aligned with these future intentions.

The Henry Ford quote, "If you think you can, or you think you can't, you're right", captures the power our thoughts have in our lives.

Jase Dreger

There's a story I came across when I was growing up. It was about a father who had two young boys who ended up in prison. Some may say they were largely a product of their own environment, and the boys' destiny was already mapped out from a very young age. Both had the same parents, a father who was an alcoholic, followed the same path as their father, grew up in the same environment, and logically would be destined to repeat the cycle.

However, one son, in his later years, chose to break the cycle by turning his upbringing and the lessons learned from his childhood and time in prison into creating positive opportunities for himself and his family.

Why did one grow up to create a life of abundance, while the other continued along living a life of scarcity? I would argue it had to do with their individual mindset. While both may have posed the question, 'What else am I supposed to do with my life?' they received very different answers.

Our mindset is often influenced by the way we interpret a situation, which is based on our perceptions, beliefs and attitude.

Inside every challenge or difficult period in my life, I've always sought to reframe a situation, to figure out if I could turn my adversity into an opportunity.

Through all of life's adversities, have a mindset that's underpinned by a strong self-belief, such as trusting that you're worthy of happiness, love and success, and you deserve to have a life of abundance.

I think humility and knowing that you don't have to get it right all the time, while remaining open to learning new things about life and yourself, is so important.

I often admit to my boys that I don't have it all together, but I'm working hard to make a difference in how I decide to live for them and others.

I choose to add value through the work I do, and I feel incredibly blessed to be surrounded by people who do the same.

What's the best way people can achieve a great life-work balance?

They need to discover their highest values and then identify whether the work they do and where they spend their time and energy are aligned. It's not a matter of doing more of something or working harder to achieve a different outcome. It's about finding joy in the things that propel us forward and eliminating those aspects of our life that do the opposite.

My eldest son's responses to a question asked during his acceptance interview to attend secondary college, captures this idea perfectly. He was asked to identify and explain what he thought were his strengths and weaknesses. He said, "My strengths are that I'm good at identifying and doing the things I'm good at doing, and my weaknesses are that I'm good at identifying and not doing what I don't enjoy".

I don't like to over-complicate things, so I find myself doing more of what I love and less of what I don't.

My advice is to declutter, identify your roles, responsibilities, and highest values, maintain a good mindset, put an accountability/action-oriented plan in place and overcome self-limiting beliefs.

Why is mindset important?

Mindset governs the choices we make and those we don't. It influences our actions and behaviours. It drives our emotions, reactions to others and whether we allow the smallest obstacles to slow us down or propel us forward. It points us in the direction of our goals, how quickly we achieve them, and the lessons learned along the way.

Mindset governs our attitude and how we approach every moment of every day, as well as the relationship we have with ourselves and other people. It can lead us to a life of joy and excitement or feeling overwhelmed and in despair. It impacts where we spend our time and energy. A strong mindset can often be the difference between overcoming adversity and helping us realise our potential, or allowing self-doubt and fear to prevent us from taking action.

How does visualisation help aid your performance?

Visualisation involves mentally rehearsing a future event and is a staple of many elite athletes and entrepreneurs. It enhances performance, because it enables you to have a safe space to practise what you want to achieve. The best way to do this is to remain still and imagine going through the process of the action, using all five senses.

By repeatedly practising your desired outcome through visualisation, you stay focused on the small steps that will help you reach your goals. Meditation is a great supplement to visualisation, as it helps calm the mind and turns off the distractions and negative voices.

Through visualisation and meditation, you can find solutions to your problems, develop better outcomes and connect to your true purpose.

Is meditation or mindfulness something everyone should practise?

Meditation is everything it's cracked up to be and more. Everyone should at least try it and maybe give it one more chance if they didn't find it helpful the first time. You don't have to spend a lot of time. Even five minutes is enough.

Meditation is the gift that keeps on giving. The more I meditate, the deeper I can go, and the more I get out of the state of relaxation. This is critical for anyone with an active mind.

How can people be happier in life?

People can be happier in life by following these seven steps:

1. Have a positive attitude.

    See the best in others, adopt a can-do attitude, refuse to give up or give in, and be easy to get along with.

2. Don't expect everyone to think or behave life you do.

    Lose your sense of entitlement and rigidity. Don't expect everything to be done a certain way.

3. Practise patience.

    Give yourself and others permission to make mistakes.

4. Serve others.

    Advocate for those who may not be able to advocate for themselves.

5. Build self-confidence.

    Continue doing the basics and keeping promises to yourself and others.

6. Enjoy the small pleasures of life.

    Take the dog for a walk, have a coffee, listen to music, cook a favourite meal or catch up with friends.

7. Fall in love with learning.

    Always be willing to learn something new, even if it doesn't fall within your area of interest.

How can people be healthier?

To be in a state of good health requires more than just being active and eating well.
There are a number of key elements to living healthy.

1. Take responsibility for your own health.

    Don't outsource your health to someone or something else. For instance, when you're in pain, rather than reaching for medication, make sure you regularly hydrate yourself, maintain good posture, and take the time to relax and unwind through music or meditation.

2. Get regular health checks.

    Peace of mind is knowing what's going on inside of you. Prevention is better than the cure.

3. Implement a daily self-care routine.

    It will help to avoid or reduce accumulative fatigue.

4. Have fun.

    Enjoy what you do, be kind to yourself and others, and find a creative outlet.

5. Challenge yourself.

    Make small changes at least once a week.

6. Declutter.

    Out with the old and in with the new or nothing at all. Start filling your life with things that are aligned with your highest values.

7. Talk to someone when you're not feeling okay.

    Never suffer in silence. Remember that you are much loved, you matter, and there's always someone who believes in you.

What is your simple formula for health?

- ❖ **Movement**

    Exercise, stretch or engage in a fun activity.

- ❖ **Nutrition**

    Choose colour over calories, limit consumption of alcohol, sugar and packaged food. Eat according to what's right for you.

- ❖ **Mindfulness**

    Walk in nature, using all of your senses.

- ❖ **Meditation**

    Sit in silence, calming the mind, and connect with the Universe.

- ❖ **Laugh**

    Have a sense of humour about yourself and your situation. Laugh, smile and be a part of something bigger than yourself.

We need to focus on our physical well-being, our family, where we are financially and our vocation, in order to achieve fulfillment. It helps to assess which areas we're optimising and where we may need to devote more of our attention.

Our highest values will help guide us. Many of us wind up being in a state of unhappiness or perceive we're less than, because we put a greater emphasis on one area of our life over the other. We need to accept that we can't always be in a state of fulfillment all the time. We can, however, aspire to be at a higher level across each area than we previously thought possible by solely resting on one domain. It's a bit like diversification with investments. Don't put all of your eggs in one basket, because you run the risk of losing everything.

The key to good health is understanding the integral relationship between head, heart and mind.

Why is health important?

Health is central to our overall wellbeing and state of happiness. It involves every part of the body and influences how we think, feel and behave.

What is the one message you wish to share with the world?

You are seen. Everyone matters. We all have our own unique gifts, or as I like to call them, 'superpowers'. Often, this becomes our life purpose, which allows us to find meaning and clarity, and helps us connect with our higher self.

If you're going through a turbulent time, a period of real disruption, then make sure you extract every single bit of wisdom you can. Always ask yourself what the lesson is. What is this situation trying to teach you?

Well-being is made up of our physical, emotional, mental, and social health factors, all of which affect our life satisfaction and how we feel about ourselves and the world around us.
Good health is the doorway to achieving our goals and living a meaningful life.

It optimises our ability to live well, work well and retire well.

 To discover more about how Jase can help you *Elevate Your Performance*, simply visit www.elevatebooks.com/performance

Sēini F Taumoepeau

Focus Your Flow

Sēini 'SistaNative' Taumoepeau (she/her), is an orator and songwoman who practises Faivā (performance of space) and Tauhivā (relational space). She's a performance artist, presenter/broadcaster and creative industries professional, with a career spanning over thirty years.

A voice of Modern Australia, Sēini is an interdisciplinary artist, storyteller and founder of OceaniaX and LELEI Wellness.

Sēini is a veteran of the arts media and culture, as well as in the educational and personal development sectors, with an intersectional Oceanic-Pacific lens and First Nations focus.

Sēini connects with global communities. She carries medicine in her presence, hands and voice, commanding an aesthetic in harmony and rhythm, working with the invisible and intangible.

Sēini F Taumoepeau

Focus Your Flow

How important is it to feel a connection to others?

As Oprah Winfrey says, "You can either see yourself as a wave in the ocean, or you can see yourself as the ocean."

For over forty years, I've studied the art of performance and creativity and how it relates to wellness, community and communication. Over that time, what I've come to realise is that most people need to feel connected. Invariably, we call this 'love', and when we have love, we feel more wellness.

I've learned that there are unlimited ways humans practise connection, and generally speaking, most people want to feel their own special brand of love in greater quantity and quality. In my case, my special brand of love connection has always been song.

While we humans have unlimited ways we seek connection, we also have specific strategies that can help us achieve them and become aligned with what's most meaningful to us. My mission is to share strategies with people for reaching their performance goals by utilising their own special brand of love, in order to become even more connected and aligned with what is most meaningful to them.

Or to use Oprah's words, I want people to see themselves less like a wave and more like an ocean.

What do you mean by having a special brand of love connection?

I've workshopped, taught and performed live for small, intimate gig rooms, outback school classrooms, on the back of trucks in regional towns and Australia's largest arenas and outdoor amphitheatres. I've been onstage in front of thousands of people and stood alone in a radio studio broadcasting live to international audiences. So I can tell you that the most direct way I can share my vibe, my frequency and my personal light with people, is by using my voice live, amplified through a microphone. Sometimes I sing, sometimes I talk and sometimes I share others' songs and stories. It's all become one and the same.

That's my special brand of love connection. It's instant, and it's real.

The way I know this is through audience feedback and also feedback from my own body. I feel lighter and in tune when I resonate with others using my voice and my body as my instrument to communicate. Whether they're in a live audience or at an international distance, there are signs they also feel connected.

It's a deep privilege to hold the attention and focus of others, and I feel deeply grateful for that honour to connect, especially in real time.

Have you ever heard the phrase 'feeling lifted?' Well, that's what it feels like. It's as if there's a new elevated frequency, where there's more room to move, and we've collectively created it together. At times it can be experienced as joy, but mostly it feels magnetic, like there's no static. In the end, I feel satisfied, fully aware and in balance.

That's what I mean by my special brand of love connection.

I also call it 'special', because when you locate your own frequency, people start to identify you with that vibe all the time, almost without any effort. Or rather, you feel so good about the effort you put into it, that it becomes easy and automated.

When did you first know this was your passion?

I was a young child when I saw the signs that there was passion in song. It was everywhere and in everything in my childhood. I felt it inside me, and it meant love to me.

Sēini F Taumoepeau

My origin is the Kingdom of Tonga in the South Pacific, and when I was young, singing and music were my constant companion. There were over forty people in each of the choirs who would practise complex arrangements in my grandparents' home, with the choir master keeping time by hitting a stick on the ground. I remember the massive Lali (log drum) under Grandma's huge Mango tree in our backyard, someone would play rhythms on to call everyone to choir or dance practice. I loved all of those sounds!

My grandpa built our church directly across the street, so there was constant group singing happening all around me most of the time. The church bell in the tower was so sonically exciting. We were on the islands, so the sea breeze and salt wind blew in gentle gusts from our lagoon. There was the sound of warm tropical rain hitting the tin roof, and we would run out to play with the whole village. It was like the sky was singing to us making us quiet, while the clouds wept and brought life to our soil.

There was also the beating of logs, with women making Tongan tapa and ngatu (bark cloth), and those sounds were always around.

In Tonga, everyone sings and learns to stand while they speak in public, so I've always been enamoured with having rich vocal sounds and words around me. Some of my aunty's vinyl records at the time are still my favourites, even now, such as Stevie Wonder, ABBA, The BeeGees, The Supremes and Donna Summer.

How did that initial passion grow into what you do today?

My mother and father worked in radio and were both musical, so we always had the radio on. Mum would be editing her reel-to-reel taped interviews for her show, or my father would play vinyl records and sing along. My big sister was given a tape recorder when she turned twelve, and we listened to cassette tapes of our favourite music show as we went to sleep. When we got older, our mum could borrow vinyl records from her work library that we'd hear on our favourite radio show, *The Rhythm Method*, so we had access to freshly curated popular songs.

My parents were a young professional couple who loved entertaining and taking my siblings and me to festivals and events all over the city. They put us in local piano and tapdancing lessons, ballet classes, and all kinds of sports, but most importantly, they gave us quiet downtime to read, imagine and play and listen to music and dance.

I listened to all kinds of songs and sounds, which enabled me to tune my performance ear. I would often be found asleep next to the speakers, learning songs. When I was taught new lullabies or nursery rhymes at kindergarten, I'd sing them over and over, until I cried. In retrospect, I realise that lots of nursery rhymes had beautifully sad, confronting stories.

My first Sydney Opera House choir performance was when I was in second class. I performed *Joseph and the Amazing Technicolor Dreamcoat* with singers from all over the state, and my whole family came.

My identification with song grew when I became a teenager in high school. I started taking leadership roles academically, in sports, music class, student representative council, the debate team or during the graveyard shift at my local radio station (shh don't tell my mum I snuck out). People would then associate me with my voice, my songs, my talks, or even my cheers at sports carnivals. I became known for being on a microphone or leading people using my voice in many ways, always with a song. It all had a storytelling quality to it and was my point of difference.

After high school, I went to university to study media communications and the music industry, and picked up indigenous studies as a minor, which changed the trajectory of my whole life. I joined my first band,

Sēini F Taumoepeau

Manuhiri Pasifika Women's Trio, and the rest, as they say, is her-story. We toured all around Australia, song writing and performing.

What is your greatest life lesson?

My greatest life lesson is that all sentient beings suffer and that nothing is missing. Life isn't all or nothing. It exists in balance. All life is a relationship. We need to know how to sense it, see it, understand it, and co-exist in relational wellness.

It can be difficult to imagine, and it sounds cliché, but before I learned this, I really didn't understand that suffering encompasses what it means to be alive with sentience. I also truly identified with a compartmental view of life, in that positive and negative couldn't exist at the same time. I've come to understand this is simply untrue and is a one-sided way of looking at life.

What led to you learning this lesson?

When I moved away from home to attend university in a regional town in the North Coast NSW, I really felt quite lost, because I was away from my family, my community and the city life I knew in Sydney. This is when I began learning and practising the Kahuna bodywork system, a massage-based energy medicine that originated with the Kānaka Maoli, who are Native Hawai'ians.

Conscious healing was one new way I found to connect culturally to the energy frequency of my Pacific region and my Polynesian roots. I also had my Pasifika Women's Trio. All of a sudden I had a whole new creative community and local indigenous family network. There was also my Bodywork practice with steady clients, as well as my band, and I worked consistently at events, markets and festivals. It's easy to see how something I initially perceived as a loss, ended up transforming my life for the better, placing me firmly on the path of my true purpose. I remained in Bundjalung country for many years after uni finished.

NSW North Coast is called the rainbow region and is most famous for Byron Bay and the alternative creative community scene. It was home to masses of hippies and LGBTQI+ communities in the 1980s and 90s who'd moved there seeking an alternative to living in the big urban centres. They wanted to create a more unconventional and inclusive regional life. It was beautiful, and I loved having my own small businesses, along with my song writing, healing, performing and travelling.

I'd already been interested in holistic practices due to our traditional indigenous science at home. Also, I'd learned yoga and Ayurveda from Deepak Chopra's books. I was always searching for different ways to heal my chronic full-body eczema that had been so debilitating and caused much suffering since I was a child. My best guess is that this may have been what helped make me so sensitive, inside and out.

In my first year at uni, for the first time in my life I completely healed my eczema, and it never came back.

It became a turning point in my path. Performing song and producing media were just two of the ways I connected with others. Ever since then, I've continued to study, share, and learn how to help people and communities heal in many creative ways that also synthesised my own methods along the way.

What's your most inspiring client story?

Hands down, my most inspiring story has to be my first coaching client ever, which totally took me by surprise.

My client, who I'll call 'Ofa, which means 'love' in my Tongan language, was someone I'd known very well when she signed up for coaching with a very distinct goal in mind. At that time, all of my coaching clients were academics, post-graduate students, or people in middle management or executive professional roles.

'Ofa was a creative veteran and had been teaching academically for a long time. She'd achieved her master's but decided she would get her PhD. She wanted my help keeping her confidence up and problem-solving her mindset, so she could continue being productive and successfully gain her doctorate. It all seemed straightforward.

'Ofa lived in a gorgeous one-bedroom garden flat with her kitty, which she was still paying off, and was a diligent and disciplined client in the early sessions. Her general life goals were

- PhD
- pay off flat
- care for her cat and aging mum.

Around about the seventh session, as we were steadily building great rapport, and 'Ofa was feeling incredibly confident, we hit a snag. A surprise memory surfaced while we were doing some general but deep reorganising of 'her habits of sabotage' by working on her mindset strategies.

It was at that point 'Ofa entered an old and deep memory that seemed to just float to the surface of her mind like a balloon filled with helium.

It was a turning point that rerouted not just our sessions, but 'Ofa's entire life. She confided in me about a negative long-term experience that started when she was a child. It was damaging enough to distance her from any desire for love, intimacy or partnership.

In response to this trauma, 'Ofa had simply created an entire lifestyle where she was in complete control. It made her feel safe and secure. She'd never imagined that perhaps she might consider another way of living.

'Ofa began considering online dating. After a giggly session about 'trying new things', without telling me, she did some face-to-face speed dating and then downloaded a dating app, and on her first swipe right, she matched with someone she thought was handsome. Suddenly she was dating, and two years down the track, they'd barely spent a day apart and decided they would get married. 'Ofa says that she never would have found the love of her life if it hadn't been for our coaching sessions.

I can't reveal 'Ofa's earlier trauma, but I couldn't imagine how anyone was able to survive what she went through, much less be vulnerable enough to fall in love. But with the way the heart and brain store energy, lives can be transformed when we put energy in motion and what was stagnant begins to move with momentum. I've witnessed the absolute impossible become possible for my clients, even the ones who thought they had it all.

The other interesting thing was how easily the energy flowed for 'Ofa's PhD and the lightness in the way she felt about her academic goals and achievements once she had the focus, attention and care she found through intimate love by allowing it to flow in her life.

From that moment on, my clientele began to change. I attracted more creative and family-oriented clients, as well as people who were seeking to transform their lives and lifestyles. My coaching practice, once logic-centred, became more heart-centred. This taught me that while we may use the language of logic, love and fulfilment seems to be the main driver of success and not achievement alone.

I learned so many life lessons from working with 'Ofa, and of course, I sang for her and her husband at their beautiful wedding!

> "We keep moving forward, opening new doors, and doing new things, because we're curious, and curiosity keeps leading us down new paths."
> ~ Walt Disney

What mindset do you believe is needed in order to create a great life?

I help people focus their flow, so not only do I recommend having a growth mindset, but having a curious and creative one as well.

It's important to be someone who's open to possibilities and welcomes the unexpected, so an attitude based on love and possibilities, not fear and hopelessness, is the main mindset shift needed to create a great life.

We're in the information age, and this means we have so much information swirling around us at all times, that being risk-averse transforms into our default setting.

Stepping into the unknown becomes a muscle we haven't worked much. It's important to understand that if you want to create a great life, you also cultivate a mindset that's able to feel safe travelling down an unbeaten path. Become comfortable with being a little bit uncomfortable and focussing on the benefits of the journey, not just the destination.

> "I am enough of an artist to draw freely upon my imagination. Imagination is more important than knowledge. Knowledge is limited. Imagination encircles the world."
> ~ Albert Einstein

Do you have an example from your own life where this mindset has been applied?

My last name is Tau-moe-peau, which literally means 'Battle with the Waves'. It's a title bestowed upon my ancestor who was a master navigator, specifically in the areas between the Kingdom of Tonga, Fiji and Sāmoa. Part of coming from an enduring culture of master navigators is that we engage the waves and the current, and see ourselves as part of the ocean, always navigating, in tune and in relationship and with our surroundings. This is how I show up in my life.

Our people settled the Moana, otherwise known as the Pacific Ocean, which covers one-third of the planet. In our corner of the Pacific, the Polynesian triangle, an area that's approximately 1,300,000 km squared, my ancestors settled lands at a ratio of 1:1000, which means for every one kilometre of land, there's 1000 kilometres of sea that are the deepest on the planet.

Up until a few hundred years ago, our people had been relatively alone in our region. This is because for thousands of years, what other people saw as a barrier or boundary, our people saw as a highway, opportunity on the horizon.

The difference was a willingness to devise relational navigation skills as a mindset technology. It allowed us to openly expand into a space the size of a third of our planet and enjoy it for ourselves for hundreds of generations, while developing enduring languages and cultures, evolving all along the way.

In order to become the greatest navigators of all human civilisation, our Polynesian people devised cultures where intelligence was no longer held in the material. It became embedded in our values, our languages and in our mindset and beliefs. A belief in ourselves and also in each other. We grew genetically strong and made our oceans our island homelands. Sometimes, to have a great life, you have to be willing to let go of everything you think you know and learn how to become who you will become.

When you realise that you're your own greatest asset and the unlimited possibilities of creativity, expansion and evolutionary opportunities that arise from this idea alone, your senses open up. Everything in the cosmos will sing to you. Then you can listen to it, understand it and perhaps enjoy singing along as well.

How can this type of wisdom apply to everyone?

I'm a huge fan of the Buddhist billionaire, Dr Kazuo Inamori, and his Success Equation. It seems basic, but it's truly an ingenious recipe for experiencing great results. I share it often with clients and students, so they have a tool they can always use to adjust their behaviour on their own, and being curious, I love to hear about their amazing results.

Briefly, what Dr. Inamori prescribes is this:

The Result of your Life = Attitude x Effort x Ability

So what you experience as the outcome of your life is the product of your attitude, effort and abilities. I feel that anyone could apply this success equation at any point in their life and get a good result.

This is the scoring system:

Effort and Ability can range from 0 to 100points
Attitude can range from -100 up to +100

By using this method, you can figure out how helpful or harmful your attitude is regarding the results you experience. For example, a person of average ability who puts in phenomenal effort with an amazing attitude, may well outperform someone of genius ability who puts in a shallow effort with a poor attitude.

What this means is that the result of your life can change by 180 degrees, depending upon your attitude.

How's that for navigational principles anyone can utilise? It's phenomenal. Dr Inamori's work goes a lot deeper, but this simple formula is so useful in an everyday capacity, and it really helps encourage people to maintain a positive mindset. Change your attitude, change your possibilities.

> "Be kind, for everyone you meet is fighting a hard battle."
> ~ Ian MacLaren (John Watkins)

Do you have an approach to your own performance?

My approach works on all kinds of performance, and it's about the art of showing up at your best in each moment.

Being a performer, as well as a creative and a live broadcaster, is a lot like being a surfer. You have to ride the waves that come and be ready in the moment when one arrives. So many things can happen, and you're basically at the mercy of the ocean. Being ready and able to catch the oncoming waves, I call being 'in flow'.

F - Frequently

L - Love

O - Organised

W - Wisdom

You've probably heard of the 10,000-hour Rule of Mastery, which is that it takes 10,000 hours of intensive practise to master any complex skill or material.

Similarly, my F.L.O.W. formula encourages you to create specific habits and rituals that will help you engage with whatever skill or material you wish to master. The goal is to ritualise and create as many touch-points as possible with your own way of creating.

You do this by combining two simple triangles of behaviour to make one star with six points. Then you ritualise and make a habit of actively enjoying organising your wisdom within each of these behaviours. When you do this, you live and are in flow with your own purpose. It's a creative cycle that keeps flowing throughout your life. As you expand in mastery and experience, your wisdom and love will grow as well.

**THE FOCUS YOUR F.L.O.W. FORMULA =
(3 WAYS YOU F.L.O.W.) + (POWER OF I.A.M)**

F - FREQUENTLY
L - LOVE
O - ORGANISED
W - WISDOM

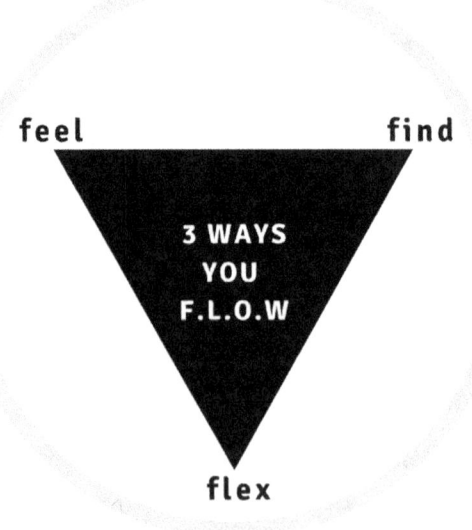

Figure 1. 3 WAYS YOU F.L.O.W Triangle Diagram

Figure 1

3 WAYS YOU F.L.O.W. (see Figure 1)

This is about how you choose to connect. I encourage you to fall in love with your flow. Become a passionate lover, while remaining fluid and committed with how you care and connect to your creativity.

1. **Feel your F.L.O.W.**

   ❖ Use all of your senses as often as you can to connect with the task.

   I'll use singing as an example. From a young age, I listened to music, which developed my 'performance ear'. I sang along to everything, I played with my voice, singing, speaking, whispering and manipulating it as much as I could. I did this while listening to music and also in conversations. I experimented with my environment and threw myself into the experience of singing. I used my voice in space, while listening deeply to the feelings of my body instrument and the way it all affected me personally. I loved listening to the wisdom of others and regularly added my own voice and body to the mix as often as I could.

2. **Find your F.L.O.W.**

   ❖ Locate in quantity and quality (time, space, emotion, physical conditions) your optimum connection to the task. Search for answers.

   For me, I find that quiet and solitude works best for being creative, such as if I'm composing or coming up with new ideas. I love working in studios with headphones on in remote locations. It helps me feel my feelings, think my own thoughts and tune into something unique. However, there's always the next step, collaboration, which means working with a team once the idea is solid and formulated. I love to engage with others, growing the idea into something real that can be shared with other creatives.

3. **Flex your F.L.O.W.**

❖ Showtime: Share the task with witnesses.

You must show the idea to others who aren't involved in the creative process. It may be a pitch, a small gathering or even just one or two people. You could also choose to post it somewhere. The idea grows into a new life once it has witnesses, so the sooner you do this task, the sooner the idea begins its own life of growth and connection.

> "I paint flowers, so they will not die."
> ~ *Frida Kahlo*

POWER OF I.A.M. (see Figure 2)

Have you heard of Enheduanna? She's the world's first known author-poet, an ancient Sumerian princess and high priestess of the Goddess Inanna. Though she isn't well known in the modern world, her influence can still be seen everywhere. I mention her now because of the way she added autobiographical context to sacred knowledge, and for the first time, publishing it in stone. The power of incantation and the words 'I Am', as well as her published works on calcite stone and its effect on humanity, can be utilised to help us along our own creative journey.

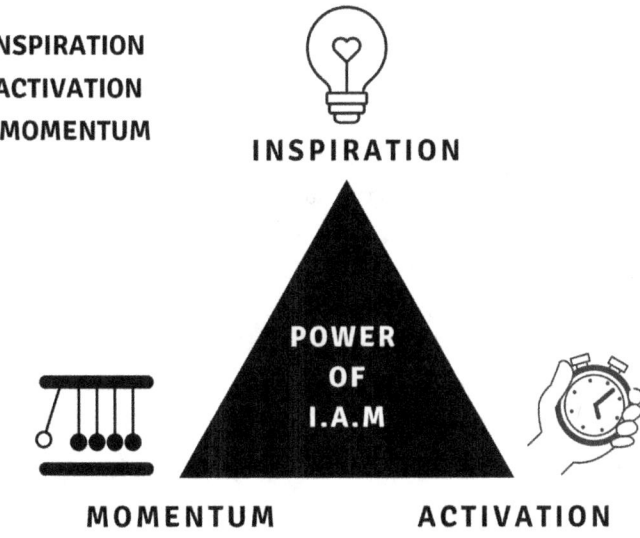

Figure 2. POWER of I.A.M Triangle Diagram

Figure 2

In our Focus Your F.L.O.W. formula, I.A.M. stand for three enactive approaches that make the incantation work:

1. **Inspiration**

❖ Tune into your idea.

   This enaction is about doing everything you can to nurture your idea and get it into a mode that allows it to manifest and change form. Using my example of singing or song writing, I often write my ideas down on paper or use my phone note-taker. I also record myself singing when inspiration hits, or sometimes I tell someone the idea when I'm working collaboratively, so it can be workshopped.

2. **Activation**

❖ Make your idea 'in real life'.

This enaction is about creating the 'because' part of the 'I am' incantation. These are the series of actions a creative takes that makes things happen. For example, saying out loud, "I am a singer and songwriter, because I practise singing daily. I know one-hundred songs by-heart, and I write down, record and practise every new song idea twenty times a week".

3. **Momentum**

❖ Make your idea move. *Momentum* $p = mv$ *mass x velocity.*

Momentum is the quantity of motion created by the mass multiplied by the speed. This enaction is about your idea having a ripple effect. For example, in writing a new song, I may record my idea and send it to a fellow musician or producer. I might then add even more sounds to it and give the idea even more form and structure. I may name it and perform it for a few people and get some feedback. I will also make lots of decisions and actions based on the wisdom I've been collecting to inform all of these decisions, knowing that momentum also creates even more momentum. One song may be the start of a series or finding alignment with other projects.

> "I know nothing with any certainty,
> but the sight of stars makes me dream."
> ~ *Vincent Van Gogh*

THE FOCUS YOUR F.L.O.W FORMULA (see Figure 3)

The 3 WAYS YOU F.L.O.W. triangle and the POWER OF I.A.M. triangle together create a six-pointed Star Cycle.

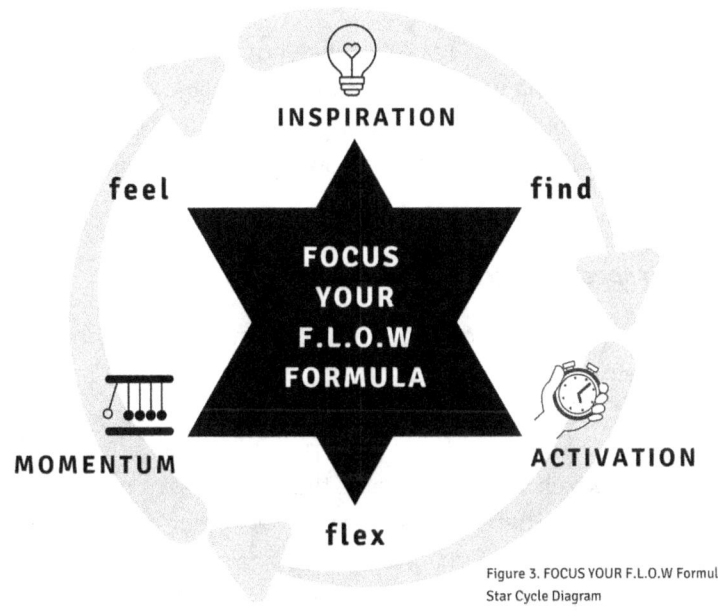

Figure 3. FOCUS YOUR F.L.O.W Formula Star Cycle Diagram

Figure 3

This is where the FOCUS element becomes the dominant practice. Your F.L.O.W. depends upon the act of moving between two polarities and finding balance. Along this cycle, you will find that each step in the formula is different, depending on a great many variables, just like surfing. Anything is possible, some great, and some not so great. Remember, life isn't all or nothing. It's not one-sided, but in balance. Everything co-exists in relationship to one another.

So we use this star to navigate our way, knowing that we float along the tension lines between the polarities. What I mean is that we do everything we can to act in sequence and make decisions that keep energy moving through our ideas, and we trust in the sequence by loving organised wisdom.

To use my example, singing is allowing your voice to cascade and fall, soar and fly, dancing with music and space. It can be harsh and tense or soothing and nurturing. Even though you can't see the voice crafting the sound, you feel it, and song is a powerful force when you encounter it.

Is there a specific principle you live by?

If I had to choose, I would say that I live by a synthesis of three sources, like a threefold braid woven together.

The first is the name of my maternal ancestral home in Tonga, Tauta'ehoko, which means 'The battle that never was'. It's a metaphorical historic reference that serves as a reminder of our people's resilience and the importance of the way we remember history. The stories we hold and what we use to define ourselves are important. They're instrumental in how we view our potential and choose our focus. They determine everything we perceive and experience, and how we place ourselves in time.

The second is a popular quote by martial arts star Bruce Lee, who I was introduced to at Tauta'ehoko, where my grandfather held movie nights for the village, often interpreting the narration, performing the voiceover as a skilled orator and adding local humour to it. Martial arts movies had taken the Pacific by storm in those days, and even as a baby I could feel the buzz they created. It helped me decide to one day become a capoeira martial artist and am now training in Lo Ban Pai (spiral energetics).

Bruce Lee's films introduced me to the awesome power of storytelling through media and new technology, but mostly the power of storytelling from different cultures and a dedicated practice to expanding human potential.

This is the quote that inspired me:

"You must be shapeless, formless, like water. When you pour water in a cup, it becomes the cup. When you pour water in a bottle, it becomes the bottle. When you pour water in a teapot, it becomes the teapot. Water can drip and it can crash. Become like water, my friend".

The third is the book of my Lo Ban Pai teacher, Lujan Matus, called *The Power of Emptiness: Being, Knowing and Not-Doing*.

This book is about learning through daily devoted practice, the power of the present moment and the art of being fluid, devoted and focussed on living heart-centred. Learn to be creatively inspired and creative in the current, without holding onto old stories. Allow new potential to flow through alignment and in its own season. That's the way I focus and live my own flow.

 To discover more about how Sēini can help you *Elevate Your Performance*, simply visit www.elevatebooks.com/performance

Dr Dimitra Mersinia
Achieving Holistic Performance

Dimitra (Demi) Mersinia has been a health professional for over 25 years who combines coaching, mentoring and consulting in the field of health and wellbeing. She also uses her vast skillset to assist healthcare workers and other professionals perform at their best.

After witnessing her father's passing due to doctor error, Demi trained as a doctor, a dentist and a neuroscientist, before entering the fascinating world of body and brain health.

Demi sees the mouth as the gateway to general health and seeks to demystify the medical jargon often thrown at patients, to get to the root cause of the problem. Her purpose is to leave her patients smiling, knowing they're following a program tailored just for them.

Demi maintains her smile by connecting with people, travelling, photography and making jewellery.

Dr Dimitra Mersinia
Achieving Holistic Performance

What does the word performance mean to you?

Life is a continuous daily performance through the roles we've chosen for ourselves.

In one context, it can mean displaying the best version of ourselves at work, at home and within the community, as well as in our social interactions.

We also rate our performance in terms of our achievements, which give us a sense of accomplishment, whether in our personal or professional life. By striving to improve ourselves, we validate our direction towards a greater vision and purpose, and raise ourselves to a higher standard that we live by and pass on.

Our performance can be affected by our level of physical and mental preparedness, and by our energy, thoughts, environment or underlying health issues.

We're at our best when we

- feel inspired
- have a sense of responsibility (such as protecting the family)
- have direction and feel motivated
- are healthy, energised and have clarity of purpose.

We perform at our worst when we

- have no direction or hope
- lack clarity or have brain fog
- feel overwhelmed and have a constant sense of anxiety.

Our self-assessment or critique of our performance is measured by our completed tasks, levels of energy, whether we feel good or drained and a personal sense of accomplishment, and therefore, self-confidence.

In your experience, what influences performance?

Performance is influenced by

- your mindset, which has to do with clarity, focus and planning
- your physical state, which has to do with your overall health performance (or state of wellness)
- your environment, which has to do with physical or mental clutter, social network, or altered genetic components, also known as epigenetics.

Epigenetics relates to how behaviours and environment can cause changes that affect our genes (chemical tags within our DNA that can switch genes on and off). The DNA is not altered, and the changes are reversible.

Our DNA can carry the memories of previous habits. For example, as a baby in the womb, you're inside a soup of information, not only from your parents, but also from previous generations. So you may end up being a smoker and prone to obesity and diabetes, because someone in your family was, or you might carry the risk factors to express them.

The chemical tags of DNA are affected by age, lifestyle and unhealthy states.

Epigenetic changes can also influence the growth of neurons and modify their activity through our thoughts, moods and mental health issues.

Once you become aware that this may be a component of certain behaviours, it can be changed.

Epigenetic changes can be altered by

- exercise (changes in the DNA on muscle fibres)
- food/diet, which can turn on and off certain genetic markers that play a role in health outcomes
- changes in lifestyle, which can affect the imprinting for future generations.

All of these are affected by our energy levels due to our sleep and nourishment habits.

How did you get involved in health and dentistry?

When I was nine years old, I lost my dad to a doctor's error.

While watching my mum go through a depression spiral, I spent a lot of time with my uncle, an oral physician and dental surgeon in the army. I learned early on about how your overall health was linked to your oral health and mindset. I listened to people's stories and came to appreciate how health and pain made people feel, and the impact it made on their daily lives and persona.

Being in the medical health field meant doing my best to ensure that nobody would experience medical errors. However, due to family pressures, I took a journey through different careers for a while, from an economist in the EU and U.S multinational corporates, to being a humble neuroscientist working on degenerative diseases and pain, to helping out as a clinical consultant in remote communities with the MSF and also working in public and private hospitals around Australia.

When I settled in my own practice, I was grateful I could utilise a lot of different skills that would help me run a business while contributing to the health and smiles of my patients.

What courses did you take that prepared you for your health consultancy and coaching business?

I've completed neuroscience, medical and dental studies, and received fellowships in special care dentistry and pain management. I've also studied economic, business and social policies for regional areas.

I've taken results coaching with Authentic Education, as well as health and wellness coaching.

I'm also a member of ICF, HCANZ, Lifestyle Medicine and MHFA.

Health consultancy, mentoring and coaching, are also incorporated into my dental plans. These aspects are also offered to other medical and allied health centres, which helps health professionals look after themselves, so they can look after others. It's also extended to education systems coping with mental health stresses and to other patients to help them make sense of the medical advice or information they've received.

What was your worst experience, and how did you overcome it?

There was a time when I believed I only had bad experiences.

I first thought my world crashed at the age of nine, when I lost my dad. I grew up with my mum being depressed due to having lost her soulmate and becoming a single mum overnight.

Dad had left a few debts, and while bullying was happening to me at school, I started earning pocket money by selling my glass paintings.

When I moved to London, on my second day there I got hit by a car and suffered neck and back injuries, but I had to keep working to earn my keep and learned to live with chronic pain.

After my best friend died in a car accident, I got into an abusive relationship that was very difficult to get out of. When I finally did, I had to leave my home and live in my car, one month before my neuroscience master's exams.

A lot of other incidents followed on and off for a few years, until there came a time when everything came crashing down on me. I reached my lowest point and thought there was no reason for me being around. I knew enough about meds and how they worked, so I decided to plan my exit. My main concern was leaving my mum with all the messes I'd created, so I started getting my affairs in order.

But the more I got involved in organising my life, something else was happening. I would look back at certain events and ask myself, *Why did I do that?* and *Could I have done this a different way?* To my mind, if I went through with it, I would be another 'sad immigrant' who just gave up.

I grew up existing in survival mode, with the view of pleasing others and not rocking any boats. I was always the obedient, quiet Greek girl. But from this point on, I started thinking for myself and decided to rectify some of my past life choices.

After going through this process, I came up with a way to overcome your worst experiences:

1. Have a plan A, a plan B and a plan C, but at the same time, be flexible and ready to accept what might happen in the process of any crisis.

2. Focus on one action at a time, and follow it through to the end. And if it doesn't work, take another action.

3. Reflect, and keep asking yourself questions, There's always room for improvement, and you're always in training.

4. Do things for others from time to time. Give without expecting a return. You don't know how it might help them.

I'm passionate about my work and put everything I have into it. When I felt I wasn't living up to my own expectations, I would get angry with myself and others. I became exhausted chasing the perfect outcome and started making small mistakes. I became forgetful and stopped caring. I was burnt out.

The way this manifested was that I was in pain for six months with a pinched nerve on my neck, three bulging discs and a numb arm. Plus, I soon discovered a lump in my neck. Was that a major kick in the pants or what?

Follow these steps, but look after yourself first, so you can take care of others later.

What drives and inspires you to help others?

My past experiences, with all the traumas and challenges, as well as the good times. I began a healing journey that included a lot of self-discovery, valuing and regaining my health, body and mind, with powerful and strategic regimes.

I discovered that everything is 'figure-out-able' and love passing on all the experiences and values I developed, both physical and mental, to help others on their journey of discovering their passions and re-igniting their life.

Dr Dimitra Mersinia

How is dental health connected to someone's overall health?

There seems to be a kind of divide between the medical and dental professions.

Dentistry seems to be mostly associated with 'drilling and filling', and other related mechanical and purely cosmetic aspects of treatment. Dentists have been overlooked by the profession and the community as being an 'oral physician'.

Even Wikipedia has got it right, though:

Dentistry, also known as dental medicine and oral medicine, is a branch of medicine that consists of the study, diagnosis, prevention, and treatment of diseases, disorders and conditions of the oral cavity (the mouth) commonly in the dentition (development and arrangement of teeth), as well as the oral mucosa, and of adjacent and related structures and tissues, particularly in associated maxillofacial (jaw and facial) area. The field of dentistry or dental medicine includes teeth, as well as other aspects of the craniofacial complex, including the temporomandibular joint and other supporting, muscular, lymphatic, nervous, vascular, and anatomical structures. The practitioner is called a dentist.

Dentistry was the first specialisation of medicine...The modern movement of evidence-based dentistry calls for the use of high-quality scientific research and evidence to guide decision-making, such as tooth conservation...dealing with oral diseases such as tooth decay and periodontitis, ...teeth deformities..., as well as systemic diseases such as osteoporosis, diabetes, coeliac disease, cancer, HIV, haematological diseases, cardiology....

Our role as dentists is to embrace prevention and not have a solely surgical approach. Oral health is an essential part of our general well-being. Dentists are also trained in nutrition, as the mouth is the gateway to the gut and overall health.

However, we can be quite restricted, either within hospital settings by the administrators, or in large practices by health funds, as well as what rebates a patient is entitled to, in terms of what treatments we can offer. Preventative consults, oral hygiene and diet coaching, and smoking cessation counselling, are mostly not covered. In many cases, the rebates become the sole factor for deciding which treatments or advice are accepted.

What do dentists actually do?

From the moment you walk into a dental practice, an assessment is made of your gait, posture, symmetry of your face, any blemishes (age or liver spots), moles, the way you speak and smile, and your demeanour.

So, within ten minutes, we know a lot about you!

Anything that may be happening in the body, such as general inflammation or diabetes, we can detect in the mouth and vice versa.

We feel around your neck for inflamed lymph nodes and assess for any clicks and jaw joint noises.

We assess if you're breathing correctly, which could correspond with sleep issues, your cheeks for changes in colour, your tongue for vitamin deficiencies, your saliva for dehydration issues that could lead to dental infections, and finally the gums. It's only when this assessment is completed that we get to your teeth.

Eastern medicine connects the teeth to different organs, which is often referred to as meridian charts. They're not used for diagnosis but as a catalyst for asking exploratory questions about a person's overall health.

The principle is that often an infection in the body will be mirrored to a corresponding tooth. Teeth are nourished by nerves, and the nerves are interconnected.

Infected teeth aren't something you can see or necessarily feel if the nerves inside a tooth have died. People usually wonder why if they're not in pain, they still need to come in. The problem is when the slightest niggle or pain starts, the damage has already been done. It's more pleasant, and less costly, to prevent any complications by coming in for your six-month check-ups.

There are times when the nutrients from even the healthiest foods can't get absorbed. A chronically infected tooth can cause lymphatic drainage issues and release toxins into the bloodstream that can lead to chronic inflammation.

Dental infections and tooth wear can be a manifestation of gut or thyroid issues. There are about seven-hundred species of bacteria swimming happily around the mouth. Some are good and some are not so good, and they're all looking for the opportunity to invade any empty space they come across. The opportunities arise when you miss one night of brushing your teeth, neglect to clean between your teeth, or overload on sugary treats. The bad breath you're experiencing is the happy poo of those competitive bugs that flow through your bloodstream and can be linked to heart and lung disease, diabetes, cancer and Alzheimer's.

Considerable stress, either physical or emotional, can affect the health of the gums and teeth, and your only indication may be a spot of bleeding when brushing or flossing.

Temporomandibular joint disorders (TMJD) can often go undiagnosed, which can be dangerous, because it's a very real and painful issue. You may have been given a mouthguard; but this only protects the teeth and doesn't necessarily address the root of the problem.

In a single session with a patient, we dentists play different roles. We act as psychologists, coaches, artists, engineers and chemists. We're also good stress and time managers, cleaners, and assessors. We're perfectionists.

So, the next time you go to the dentist, and you're asked about your medical history or any medications you're taking, don't hesitate to disclose everything, as it's all connected. Also, when your dentist asks you to have certain blood tests or liaise with your medical practitioner, be curious and open to learning about your body.

How do you help change people's lives?

I have a holistic practice where I approach health with the belief that everything is connected. Health is your wealth. I integrate dentistry with medicine and neuroscience, and also coach people into optimising their health, so they can perform better in all areas of their lives.

Your body works as a system. When one part is out of balance, it can cause a whole range of unexpected symptoms throughout the body.

Our thoughts, beliefs, and the stories we tell ourselves can get misaligned during challenges. They get stored in our cells and neurons in the form of inflammation, which can bring about brain fog and fatigue. Disruptions in energy levels, such as experiencing sadness, depression or anger, can cause disruptions in other areas. You can think of these as different pieces of disconnected information.

I help connect all the dots and fine tune the different aspects of behaviour, diet, and lifestyle, while giving you the tools to keep them connected and maintained for peak performance. When someone comes into a dental practice, it's a bit of a different consultation than the usual dental visit. We go through an extensive analysis of your health and how your body is performing overall. We look at sleep patterns, eating habits and mental state. We also assess where you are currently with your oral health by liaising with your medical practitioner for blood tests, scans, etc., which act like performance indicators of your blood cells, liver, kidneys and heart. We also help determine what you need and where you'd like to be.

Your treatment involves using technologies such as ozone and laser therapy, and you experience these dental treatments in a stress-free environment with special neuro-acoustic software known as Nucalm technology.

During your visit, we'll discuss coping mechanisms for relieving stress. You'll learn about your neurotransmitters, the language of the brain, and how to keep them at optimal levels for better performance.

Finally, we'll discuss maintenance of your smile, and we'll provide you with a smiles kit that includes all of the necessary tools that apply to your lifestyle and particular circumstances.

Your health program is applied by using key performance indicators of health and well-being, nutrition, sleep and hygiene habits, structural performance, and mindset.

The M.I.N.D. program was devised to help you realise what's happening within your body and to demystify confusing health information.

M	Mindset
	Manage your environment (physiological, personal).
I	Instigate/Improve habits in terms of sleep, movement and breathing.
N	Nourish the gut, mouth and mind.
D	Direct the mind and heart

The M.I.N.D program incorporates a 'lifestyle medicine plan' we call O.P.T.I.M.I.S.E.

This stage goes through a personal 'SWOT' analysis, which means looking at your *strengths*, *weaknesses*, *opportunities* and *threats* to identify where you are currently and what gaps need to be closed in order to spring clean your health and wellbeing.

Personal SWOT analysis 　　　　Spring-cleaned health

FROM		TO
Overwhelmed and/or Overstretched	O	Optimistic outcomes
Pressure	P	Purpose and priorities with values
Traumatised (physical + emotional)	T	Train with tasks and goals
Insensitive (Feeling numb)	I	Insightful and reflective
Mingled thoughts	M	Meaningful life, mental health
Inability to cope	I	Improved coping skills
Stressed	S	Satisfied, having personal strategies.
Enfeebled	E	Emotional clarity, engaged, energy management

The following is a summary of the lifestyle medicine plan and is based on the pillars of health: eat well, sleep well, think well, breathe well, move well.

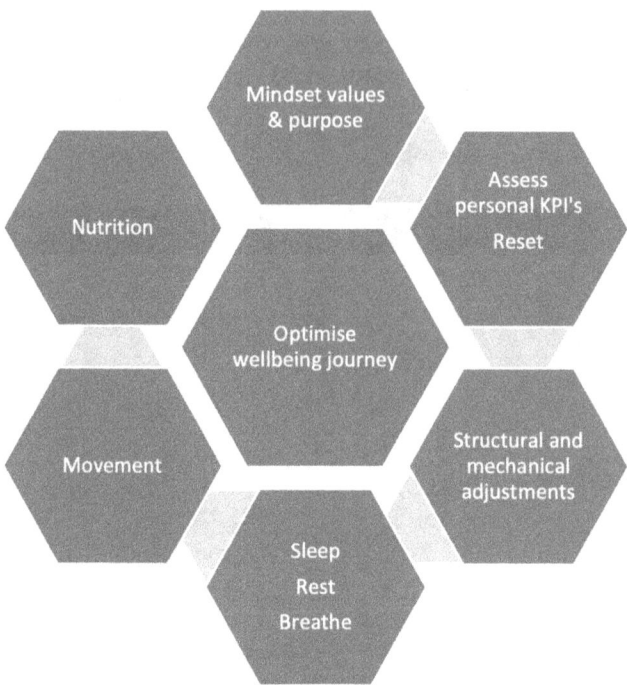

Why is health important, and how does someone know if they're in peak health?

Health is our true wealth.

When we're in a healthy state we perform at our best. When we're not well, physically or mentally, we may feel slower and a bit more scattered.

Being well is different to everyone. That's why 'Dr Google' can't always tell you the real state of your health, as it's based on other people's experiences; which are recipes that worked for them. However, it can help you become aware of a situation that you can discuss with your health professional.

To figure out if you're in peak health, you need to assess these four areas:

1. **Your physical health.**

   Have a general blood screen. This will give you an indication of how you're doing physically and if your internal cogs are in working order. Your health professional will help you interpret the results and give you the big picture. Ask questions about your thyroid levels (your metabolism), how well the big engine in your body is performing, how your liver is doing and if your kidneys are filtering well. This should all be looked at in conjunction with your vitamin and mineral levels.

2. **Your oral health.**

   Gum health is one of the important indicators of general health. Gum disease is silent, and if it's not addressed, the smallest point of inflammation can start a cycle of problems. Also, your saliva and acidity levels are connected to your gut health.

3. **Your mental health.**

   We're naturally self-obsessed. We keep wondering who we are, what we should do and how others see us. We live and tell our own stories all the time. Reflect on your thoughts and the feelings they bring up, and how these in turn, affect your daily habits. Negative self-talk can create physical problems, while positive self-talk, coupled with brain foods and movement, can neutralise the negative and bring the body and mind into balance.

Specific emotions have their own distinct patterns of neuroactivity. There's a way to regulate your emotions through re-appraisal of your experiences and changing the meaning of events.

Below are some of the neurotransmitters, which are the language of the brain. They transfer information throughout the body, between neurons and muscles.

- Dopamine, which is our reward system.

- Glutamate, which stimulates neurons to act on command.

- Adrenaline, which is responsible for our fight or flight responses.

- Serotonin, which works mainly in the gut/small intestine. It checks appetite and influences feelings of well-being and happiness.

- Oxytocin, which is the 'love' hormone.

- GABA, which calms the mind.

All of these work together and are directly connected to our overall well-being. They need healthy foods, hydration, vitamins, correct breathing, movement and restful sleep to function at their best.

4. **Your repair and regeneration habits.**

    Even on a day when you decide to do nothing, you shed thousands of skin cells a minute, which your body regenerates. You also produce one third of a gallon of saliva. The heart pumps around 1.5 gallons of blood per minute; and you generate two million red blood cells per second. In order for these systems to perform efficiently, good-quality sleep is essential, so assess your sleep hygiene and mindfulness.

Why is mindset important?

Your frame of mind is important for getting you through any situation.

When you're facing a challenge, your fear might not let you see the big picture, so you over-analyse facts, trying to find reasons not to do something or procrastinate.

Your mind is trying to find the reasons something you want to do won't be safe, so you keep asking the 'what if' questions and create stories. You may run through all the times you didn't perform well instead of seeing all the times you did.

When we're younger, it's easier to take more risks, because we don't have a history of making mistakes. However, though we may take action quicker, when looking at the big picture, we can see where putting more thought into it might have been a better choice.

How can having pillars help someone maintain focus?

In a crisis, we tend to look for a pillar to hang onto, something solid that will offer us stability through familiarity. Health professionals are supposed to always be that pillar.

When I was facing my health challenges due to burnout, I found myself wanting to stop everything, but like everyone else in my profession, I had to go to work, smile and try to calm everyone down. My work became my pillar, so I could be one for my patients and keep on going, no matter what was running in the background.

In order to do this, I had to learn how to slow down, remove myself from the stressful situation and reassess all of my vital activities, so I used the tools from the lessons I acquired from similar experiences.

However, nobody can do this alone. In a challenging situation, your mental health can become compromised and play tricks on you, and you wind up living in your head all the time, only hearing your stories. You need someone to help you see through your stories and understand how to turn them to your advantage.

How do you know if you're performing at optimal levels?

You're at your best when you're focused. You're in the flow, feeling energised, knowing what you're going to do next. You're enjoying social interactions and remain dedicated to improving your skills.

You're not performing at your optimal levels when you're feeling lethargic or overthinking. Do you feel frozen when you're about to start a task? Have you become forgetful? Do you take on too much, so your productivity has decreased, and you always wish you had just one more day to complete your tasks?

From time to time, it's good to evaluate all areas of your life and measure it with the performance indicators you've decided to utilise, in the same way you'd measure the performance of your car, your stocks and shares or your garden.

In order to get answers, you need to come up with quality questions to ask yourself. Here are some examples:

- How is my overall health?

- What are my sleep habits?

- How much nourishment have I had today (including carbs and protein)?

- Am I reacting to people in a healthy way?

- When I receive a challenging comment, do I respond in a rude manner, or am I gracious and humble?

- Do I remember mostly positive or negative things about my day?
- Am I too hard on myself if I don't complete everything on my to-do list?
- At the end of my day, do I only think about what I could or should have done?

Really think about how these measurements affect you on a daily basis.

Will you start your next day angry at yourself, because your to-do list has grown due to yesterday's unfinished items, or will you be grateful for what you did manage to complete?

How can someone find their purpose?

By understanding our identity, we can in turn identify our purpose, which reignites our passions. This will increase our focus and lead to peak performance.

Take control of your environment. The world around us may not instil hope, reliability and the certainty we need, but it's important to make sure we surround ourselves with what brings us contentment and joy.

Having a clear mind supports the decision-making processes by helping to tune out distractions and obligations.

Your *brain mind* involves the neocortex and is in charge of your advanced thoughts and reasoning processes. In other words, when faced with a dilemma, it supplies the meaning you give to it.

Your *heart mind*, like the limbic system in the brain, controls your feelings. It determines what you focus on and your analysis of what you can and can't control.

Your *gut mind* helps you listen to your body's instincts and aids you in weighing the pros and cons of a situation, so you can make a balanced decision.

Assess your energy levels. Are you getting enough sleep? How are your eating habits?

For example, those who are born in western cities have different gut flora than those born in rural areas. If you live in the city and decide to become a vegetarian or a vegan, you still won't process that food properly, as your gut's mechanisms and responses are quite different. This means you'll have a hard time absorbing the nutrients, even with supplements, which has an impact on your energy levels, and in turn your sleep patterns.

Learn to become flexible. Don't create this mental space where there are no options. The only place you would be allowed to show inflexibility is when you create your non-negotiables for the day. Your priorities are for yourself and yours alone. List those items that are important for your well-being and productivity, and make sure they're aligned with your values.

Can someone reverse or improve poor performance?

At the end of each day, reflect upon your actions, and decide what you can do better next time.

In the area of health, for example, we know that exercise and eating healthy foods can act on a DNA level to imprint improved information.

So, in other words, if we flood our system with better habits, we can reverse poor performance.

What do you think people's biggest barriers are?

1. We're constantly in a state of performance anxiety, whether it's due to public speaking, social fears or deadlines.

    Life isn't a collection of unrelated events. Health issues arise from the disconnected pieces of those events. Anxiety manifests physically, and we usually ignore it. We live such rushed lives that there's no time to think about little niggles or pains here and there.

    > "Beware of the bareness of a busy life."
    > ~ *Socrates*

    Anxiety or resentment can affect the skin and saliva production, and can also cause TMJD and broken teeth or fillings from grinding and clenching. Anger can impact the heart and the liver, which becomes evident in the gum tissues. Loss of confidence manifests as gut issues, which in turn causes loss of tooth structure due to reflux or ulceration of the oral mucosa.

    When Covid first broke out, the lockdowns were meant to slow down the spread of the infection, but we essentially were forced to slow down our lives. Yet we were quick to pick up the pace again when we could.

    We feel the need to take control of our environment, to present what outwardly appears to be our best selves, so we make decisions in order to please others and validate ourselves.

2. Not enough focus on self-care.

    We forget to spend time with ourselves and instead make decisions based on our fears, desire for personal gratification and sense of duty.

3. Underlying health issues.

   These may not be entirely obvious, because we forget to listen to our bodies or ignore medical visits due to our busy lives or fears.

4. Not knowing enough about the background of a project we're trying to tackle, and therefore lack preparation.

5. External factors, like economic developments and unexpected events, such as a pandemic. These events catch us by surprise, so we're unable to pivot.

6. Maintaining our pre-conditioned response to challenges.

   Instead of adapting, we stick to what our parents or cultural backgrounds have taught us, which may not be the best way of dealing with them.

7. An inability to find our own identity.

   In effect, we may approach each obstacle with an abundance of over- or under-confidence, which sabotages our performance.

8. No motivation and a lack of interest, especially when working for a company that doesn't bring fulfilment and isn't aligned with our values.

How can we overcome these issues?

First, become aware there are issues, and recognise what they are.

Do an audit of your performance in all areas of your life and reflect upon where you can improve and where you'd like to be.

> "Excellence is never an accident. It is always the result of high intention, sincere effort and intelligent execution; it represents a wise choice of many alternatives – choice, not chance, determines your destiny".
> ~ *Aristotle*

Maintain your determination and discipline to achieve your desired outcomes. In order to do this, you need to train like you're an elite athlete in the following ways:

Mental skills training:

Performance is easy to understand, as you can measure it. Working on well-being, enjoyment and satisfaction increases anxiety and decreases anger.

Master distractions, conquer your nerves, prepare for the competition and establish what you want to achieve.

Audit your fears, desires and duties. Do a personal analysis on your strengths and weaknesses.

Physiological Training:

Test your general systems and oral health.

Assess how your body reacts to exercise, such as walking. Find out what you enjoy, and try it out for a little while. You can formulate your own specific program and test its effectiveness for yourself.

The important thing is finding ways to move every day. We're not designed to stay still. Start with five minutes of exercise, and keep increasing daily. Baby steps.

Nutritional training:

Nutrition plays a major role in performance and recovery, but each person's goals are different, depending on their age, stress level, energy level, endurance and health deficiencies and the seasons. We can't get everything we need from food, but we also don't need to keep taking supplements all the time.

It's not only about what we eat but also the timing, so find the balance for you.

Sleep training:

The restoration and repair of our cells occurs when we sleep.

Assess your sleep habits. Do you wake up during the night? Do you maintain consistency with your sleeping habits? Are you a nose or mouth breather?

The amount of sleep we need varies from person to person. Try sleeping for six, seven and then eight hours, and figure out which one makes you feel the most refreshed. If you can, try to ensure you're in bed before eleven p.m. That's when melatonin starts to work, regulating your circadian rhythms. If it's disrupted, it will lower the quality of your sleep, and the consequences become apparent only a few years down the line, when you develop heart, respiratory and endocrine issues.

Establish good sleep hygiene and routines. Try to maintain a consistent sleep/wake schedule, and have a bedtime winddown routine. Include melatonin boosters in your diet, such as walnuts, cherries, tryptophan, vitamin B6, magnesium and zinc-rich foods. Avoid disruptors, such as blue light from electronic devices, caffeine or late dinners too close to bedtime. These suppress your melatonin.

What are the best ways to find the energy for optimal performance?

Once we're in a good physical and mental health state, energy is optimised internally. To maintain this optimisation, become aware of your empowering and disempowering thoughts.

Learning is an ongoing process. Have a sense of inner growth. Reflect and become aware of how this is occurring. The world will not stay the same. It keeps changing, so we need to learn and grow with these changes.

Visualise your future self. Where do you want to be? The brain doesn't recognise whether a thought is from the past or future. It will just do its usual scans for safety. The calmer the feelings, the safer it will feel.

Does technology help us perform better?

Depending upon the areas in which we need to perform, technology can give us, to some extent, more opportunities and speed, and makes us more efficient.

However, at the same time, there's a constant flow of information and advice, especially through social media, which can disrupt our own thoughts and focus. There are a lot of opinions and approaches. There's no one-size-fits-all solution. We need the knowledge and patience to decipher the real information that could help us, and then we can use these as a conversation starter with a health provider.

> "We are drowning in information but starving for wisdom"
> ~ Tony Robbins

It's time to take control of what goes into our brain space and to edit what we hear and see, allowing only what makes sense to help us reach our goals. Be deliberate rather than getting lost in the noise of our environment and obligations of our roles as stated by others.

What are your top tips to elevate performance?

1. Edit your outcomes. Spend time getting clear on your reasons for the tasks ahead.

2. Align your strategies with your values.

3. Know your pillars, or what you personally stand for, so you can hold onto them in times of challenges. Be prepared to be flexible and adjust accordingly.

4. Be mindful of your own abilities, levels of confidence and boundaries. Do a personal SWOT.

5. Be aware of your external environment and how it affects you.

6. Accept or learn that progress is better than perfection. Otherwise, you will live in a constant state to anxiety and under-perform.

7. Have daily allocated times for self-care, worry time and happy time.

8. Speak to your healthcare providers and GP about annual checks and full blood work, and your dentist regarding gum checks, headaches and worn-down fillings. Get an assessment of your nourishment and supplements.

9. Relying on finding answers on your own may divert you to therapies that aren't necessarily useful for your body. Your physicians know your history and can help you connect the dots.

 To discover more about how Dimitra can help you *Elevate Your Performance*, simply visit

www.elevatebooks.com/performance

Ivena Heald

A Sporting Life

Ivena Heald is a sports coach who's passionate about helping people discover their passion, so they can embrace their vulnerability and focus their energy where it's needed.

Being on the ladies' New Zealand tenpin bowling team gave her a unique perspective on what it took to motivate others to be their best selves.

In addition, her experience working with her parents at a women's refuge providing assistance for displaced families, set her on her pathway to improving people's lives.

Together with her husband, they created Sports Performance Academy NZ, a company dedicated to elevating people to reach their highest potential.

Ivena deeply believes in the power of change and recalibrating your mind, body and soul to learn your truth.

Ivena Heald

A Sporting Life

What is your biggest life lesson?

Be well, and be safe.

My father was brought up by an aunty in Jerusalem (Hiruharama in Māori) near to Wanganui township on the North Island West Coast of New Zealand. A cathedral was built by the Catholic Church in 1889. Mother Suzanne Aubert of France moved there to take care of the people in the surrounding area and built an orphanage for abandoned European children. My dad was schooled by the nuns, and religion made an enormous impact on him as a youth. The nuns had a strong set of rules for themselves, and one of them was making sure the children were supplied with tasty food, water, love, safety and religion. He was also taught the secrets of the Māori about how to treat people and Mother Nature with care, and to be kind to all.

Dad had a huge amount of wisdom to teach others, and most of our life skills growing up came from our parents.

The reasoning behind "be well, be safe" was to make sure we took great care of our physical body, our intellectual mind and our Soul. Dad reminded us to not lose focus of this simple life lesson and apply ourselves long enough to go the distance.

What does love mean to you?

Love is a powerful word that can generate deep emotion. I lean towards unconditional love, especially to humans and all life on this planet and the Universe. I love and appreciate with awe the wonders of our world and the shocking beauty that feeds the soul. Did you know that when you're feeling depressed, if you go sit with Mother Nature, she will calm you?

Every human being is created with the same cells. We are light and energy, and we're all connected. We want to be loved and to love, to survive in this world, to learn new things, and create and build a life. Love is an emotion worth feeling, living, and sharing.

Tip: *Think of someone you love, and then look at a stranger while imagining they are that person. Feel the love you have for the stranger. Imagine how you would feel if someone hurt them or made them happy.*

What is the one message you wish to share with the world?

Many years ago, I watched a movie called *The Secret*. I was so enthralled, that I watched it several times. I learned about the law of attraction and how energy is used to attract us to the things we want.

However, the most powerful one to me is the law of gratitude. This is the natural principle that action and reaction are always equal and in opposite directions. One cannot exercise much power without gratitude, because it keeps us connected to the creative power within us and makes us into the image of that to which we give our attention. The grateful mind is constantly fixed upon the best, so therefore it will receive the best.

A fantastic way to say thank you is to be grateful for the things we have in life, for the people around us and that we live in a beautiful world.

TIP: *Keep a daily journal, and write down all that you're grateful for. Another option is to record it on a laptop or phone and check them every so often. It will not only grow your positive power, but help you notice the energy growing within you.*

Ivena Heald

What is the best thing that has ever happened to you, and why?

Twenty-four years ago, I met my soul mate, Allan, at a banquet dinner. I hardly knew him, but he asked me to dance, as we were the only ones left at the table. It was a waltz, and I felt a strange "click" in my mind, as if I were part of a jigsaw puzzle and knew instantly this is where I belonged.

A month passed. He came to visit me and asked me to marry him.

That was the moment I wasn't afraid to decide. Sometimes things like this will happen in your life, and you need to make a choice based on instinct. Your intuition will guide you down a new road. Don't be afraid to make a detour. It's better to change or reinvent yourself than live in a stagnant world of your own making.

So I took a leap of faith and jumped, and I've never looked back. Allan gave me his protection, his allegiance, and his heart, body and soul. He gave me his unconditional love and devotion. He's put my life, happiness and welfare above his own and has cherished me all these days. I am totally devoted to him and give him back what he gives me.

What do you think is your life purpose?

To be a teacher. There were four teachers from my school days who made a huge impact on me. They were kind, attentive and nurturing with their guidance, which I took seriously, because their lessons were delivered to me with love.

I became a teacher in the workforce, training employees, and at the age of thirty-five, I also found my passion with tenpin bowling in Australia while on a holiday. After returning home to New Zealand, I immediately dropped hockey, and the bowling centre near me became my second home. I also wound up being a volunteer for the sport, starting with administration and fundraising.

When I moved to the Wellington region, I was fortunate to carry on with my passion for the sport and still do volunteer work. My husband was already a coach and a NZ national team representative, so he trained me. After qualifying as coaches for New Zealand, we travelled to the U.S.A. to seek more training experience from the Kegel Training Centre in Florida, that we'd pass on to our students back home. My passion is now totally focused on providing skills to those who want to stretch to a higher level of performance. The skills required are generic to all levels of competence for any sport.

There's an exercise called *The Bubble*, because it's for children, however it can easily be altered to suit teens, adults and seniors, by changing the activities you do inside the bubble. The children grow by doing this, and their parents agree they learn about their aura and realise they've had this protection around them since birth.

I was a weekend volunteer at a women's refuge with my mum, and I learned this exercise to help young children allay their fears.

The Bubble

- Stand and put your arms down by your sides, with a comfortable gap between your feet. Now relax.

- With your mouth closed, breathe in through your nose, and then open your mouth and breathe out. Do this two more times.

- Now look up, and suddenly you see lots of tiny sparkling stars falling out of nowhere and dropping on your head. They surround your body, go down to your feet and then under them. The stars float all around you, and they feel nice and warm.

- You love the stars. They spin softly and slowly all around you, and you know you can change the colours to your favourite ones. You feel happy.

- You then notice that you have a clear bubble around you that's keeping the stars close to you, so you can touch them, play with them, and even change some to the colours. You're so happy, you jump around inside the bubble and hum a tune. It feels great.

- Oh, no! You bumped into something. It was the corner of a table, but you don't feel a thing. Now you know that nothing can hurt you in this bubble, and you feel safe.

- As you walk among others, you notice that your bubble moves as well. You're the only one who can see it, and you feel as if you have a great big secret, something that no one else is aware of.

- You know that you can turn it off and on when you want to, as your bubble will always be with you when you want to see it.

For more advanced stages, you can change the vibration within the bubble, block out distractions or include a sound like "ohm" or your own relaxing music. You can place imaginary mirrors facing away from you or pull up any type of shield you want. Spiked warrior ones work well. This is added protection from the harsh negative energy coming at you, which is especially helpful during a tournament. But more importantly, this is the time you can learn to bring all of your senses together as one unit, where there are no distractions, reactions or judgement. Everything just exists in space, where you have a heightened awareness of everything around you being brighter and calm. Your body and mind are linked to your soul, and you're in a neutral position.

What are you passionate about?

I'm passionate about helping students/athletes in sport, elevate their mindset skills, especially in regard to focus. When you put your attention on something, you lean towards it physically and mentally, and then when you've satisfied your curiosity, your attention moves away from whatever you were looking at, touching, or listening to and moves on to something else. Whatever or whoever you put your attention on, becomes more real.

Attention Exercise

The purpose of this exercise is to become more aware of your surroundings.

1. Take a walk and occasionally stop and direct your attention on something close to you. Decide if you want more time to look, and if not, direct your attention on something far away from you, and again determine if you want to look at it longer or not.

2. Once you've decided you've looked at everything you want to, begin walking again.

   Do this exercise six times during your walk. You can do more if you choose to. It can also be done just sitting outside.

What do you think is a big problem for most people?

The first is not managing their money.

Money is just a tool. Some people have a lot of it and use it to make more. They know how to budget and invest.

But most people don't use their money wisely, merely living pay cheque to pay cheque, while others live financially over and above their income, which brings a lot of stress to the people around them. They haven't been taught how to be in control of their money, so it becomes a never-ending story of sorrow and regret, and their stress builds up.

The second is not having their goals aligned with who they are, but there is a way to figure this out.

Below is a goal-setting plan that will help you to find one that's specifically right for you, as well as select solutions for any obstacles you might have. Then you'll be able to align them with your life values.

LIFE VALUES ALIGNMENT PROGRAM

Goal-Setting Plan

This exercise will help determine the goals that are right for you in any area of your life.

Step One
On a clean sheet of paper, answer the following questions. They should get you to reflect upon the goals you should be pursuing.

1. *What excites you the most?*
2. *When are you the happiest?*
3. *What would you like to achieve in the next year?*
4. *What would you like to own by the end of next year?*
5. *What would you like to do by the end of next year?*
6. *What would you have to become to do what you want?*
7. *Where would you like to be in two years?*
8. *Where would you like to be in five years?*
9. *Where would you like to be in ten years?*
10. *What would you really like to do?*

11. *If you knew you couldn't fail, what would you attempt?*

12. *If it weren't for (describe an obstacle you feel is in the way of getting what you want), what would you do?*

Step Two
For questions three-twelve, rate each goal according to the following seven criteria, with (1) being very doubtful and (5) being very certain.

1. This goal invites your attention and interest. Thinking about it renews your strength.

2. Pursuit of the goal will produce something of value to you.

3. The goal offers benefits to others equal to your own.

4. The goal presents an opportunity for self-development and competence.

5. The goal is in alignment with a group goal.

6. The goal allows for personal creativity and a degree of self-management.

7. The goal presents an opportunity to achieve your deepest desire.

Now total your score.

If a goal scores between 25 and 35, it's probably right for you. If you have several goals that scored between 25 and 35, try to come up with a larger, more expansive goal that encompasses and aligns with one that's right for you. The purpose is to get to one specific goal that's in alignment with who you are.

If all of your goals only scored between 15 and 25, choose one to modify, and see if it can score higher.

If all of your goals scored below 15, take a few days to reflect upon the questions, and try again.

Life Values Alignment Plan

This is where you align your attention and energy with the goal you wish to achieve, and recognise that there is a path to success.

Step One
On a clean sheet of paper, make a list of your weekly activities. After each item, write (H), meaning it's helpful in achieving your goal, or (I) for impeding it.

Do the same for steps two and three.

Step Two
Make a list of your major expenses.

Step Three
Make a list of your beliefs regarding this goal.

What are the biggest mistakes people make in personal development well-being?

The biggest mistakes people make are not having a clear picture of where they want to go and for how long, not having any goals or a timeline set in place to achieve their steps, and not tracking their successes along the way. Or they have goals that don't resonate with their life values, so there's a misalignment. It would be prudent for them to link up with a personal development and well-being coach to help get them started.

At my company that I run with my husband Allan, Sports Performance Academy NZ, we help people reach their highest potential.

What elements need to be addressed regarding personal development and well-being, that not only help in sport, but life as well?

In regard to the basic foundation for personal development and wellbeing, there are three elements to address:

1. **Physical**

    The physical benefits of sport are composed of four primary qualities, known as The Four S's

    ▸ Strength

    ▸ Suppleness

    ▸ Sensitivity

    ▸ Stamina

Most learning blocks are related to a deficiency in one or more of these four key elements. To raise your potential, try to develop and integrate them into your life.

The master key that unlocks all four of these fundamental building blocks is
R E L A X A T I O N
Your ability to relax shows your willingness to trust.

Tension lacks energy, and relaxation enhances strength, suppleness, stamina and sensitivity.

Most people aren't efficient energy users. They waste it and create unnecessary muscular tension, even with simple movements like sitting in a chair, by tensing unrelated muscles.

Most of us have carried subtle tension for so many years, that we've forgotten what real relaxation is. It does little good for a coach to tell someone to relax, until they know what it feels like, and they become aware of the degree of tension they carry. An example is to stand and tense your whole body, and try jumping. Then do the opposite. Relax your whole body, and jump.

2. **Mental/Intellectual**

    The athletic experience can be represented by a journey up a mountain path, with the peak representing your highest potential. Wherever you stand on your path, it's wise to have a clear map of the terrain ahead, a way of seeing your position in relation to your goals, a view of upcoming hurdles, and an understanding of the effort required to reach the peak. Making smart goals in line with your values clears that pathway.

    Having a realistic vision and a deep awareness of your potential in any given endeavour, enables you to choose the wisest course and train for it. From a good beginning, everything else flows.

3. **Emotional**

    If you think of your thoughts and physical reality as two realities existing side by side, you will be closer to understanding their unique relationship.

    You're living simultaneously in two worlds:

    1. The inner reality of your thoughts, emotions, and attitudes.

    2. The outer reality of people, places, things and events.

Because we fail to separate these inner and outer worlds, we allow ourselves to become dominated by the outer world of appearance and use the inner world solely as a mirror for whatever happens to us. Your inner consciousness is a powerful force whose influence is felt in every aspect of your life. It's the most important part of who you are, and it's the main cause of your success or failure.

Everything at its purest and deepest essence is energy, and whenever you think, you're working within an immense amount of this energy in the quick, light, mobile form of thought.

Between the *inner reality of thought* and *the outer reality of your physical body*, up jumps a real threat that you sometimes can't control... *your emotions* (feelings). They can make or break you in any situation. Most people don't have control over their thoughts or feelings.

Everyone *can* control their physical behaviour, and this is the key that will pull them back from the cliff. But if you don't act; don't worry. Your brain will do it for you in the form of fight or flight.

Does visualisation help in your home and work life?

Yes, in the following ways:

1. The human brain talks in symbols, not words. If I said the word "orange" to you and asked you what it is, you would see a picture of the object in your mind and not the word.
2. It helps you to create routines in sport, education and life in general.
3. You can make changes by visualising something, because your mind can't differentiate between what is real and what is imagined.
4. You can learn linking systems to remember a long set of headings for an onstage presentation.
5. You can change the way you think by eliminating negative stories.

6. You can create a visualisation-linked story to remember items by making them look ridiculous, large and colourful.

What are some tools or strategies you would recommend for maintaining balance?

- Meditation
- Reading
- Yoga
- Stretching exercises
- Family gatherings
- Group meetings, such as a dinner centred around your spiritual practices, card night with friends, walking or fundraising.
- Health, happiness and spirituality.

How can people be happier?

Prioritise the most important things in life, live within your financial means, and keep yourself and your family safe. Concentrate on achieving balance in these areas of your life:

- Personal health and wellbeing
- Family
- Spiritual practices
- Career/work
- Extracurricular activities.

What is your simple formula for health?

Clean water, fruits and vegetables, sleep, exercise, work, and play.

How can people overcome fear?

I'll give you a few examples:

Example One: In the physical game of sport, its best to go through the process of different scenarios. If you're fearful of being in front of a huge crowd in a playoff against another athlete, especially at the national or international levels, practise these stepladder playoffs as much as possible, starting with a bunch of friends, and then a few athletes that are much better than you, with all of your family members watching.

If an opportunity arises in a regional or national tournament, sign up for it. Practise until you become confident, especially before you hit the high-performance playoffs.

Example Two: Listening to an audio meditation. Make sure it's catered to taking you through a scenario that embraces your fear and itemises the components of how your fear was created by looking at where it may have come from. This will set you on the road to eliminate the fear, so you can thank it and let it go gracefully, knowing it's been with you for a long while. Do this audio visualisation as many times as necessary.

What are the best ways people can find energy?

- Controlling their stress
- Not overworking
- Eating for energy
- Taking in just enough caffeine without overdoing it
- Light stretching and warming up
- Breathing exercises.

Why do you think students/athletes get overwhelmed and frustrated when playing sport?

- They don't have the mindset skills to handle any problems that come their way.

- They lose their physical process for their sport and can't get back into the game, so they become fixated on the problem, which makes it worse.

- Someone may have said something they took the wrong way, which got them angry or frustrated.

What stops people in sport from achieving the success they really want?

They may feel they don't know enough and need more education and training in some areas of their sport, so they decide to just do it socially instead of professionally.

They're distracted by other pressing matters, perhaps at home, and aren't truly focused in the moment, which is a skill that needs to be practised.

They may not be financially prepared to go the distance. Most sports require expensive equipment and lots of training.

They also may lack self-confidence and tell themselves they're not good enough, so no matter how much they practise and learn new skills, it will never be enough for them to take the leap.

Is technology helping or hindering us?

Both.

Technology has opened us up to the world via our personal computers, laptops and mobile phones.

There's more advanced technology that allows users to quickly create business and office administration programs that can be shared with others on any platform.

Most young people use their mobile phone to connect with online platforms, because it's the quickest way for them to communicate.

When COVID-19 hit, if it weren't for technology, the world would have shut down. It shed a light on how important technology is to communicate, so a fast-moving influx of entrepreneurs began creating new online businesses.

People don't necessarily need to leave their home to be entertained.

But the downside of this technology is that it could be a distraction, not only for adults but to young children who become addicted to being online. They're not connecting and building relationships face to face with friends and family, and as a result, they're growing up with little social skills, which is especially harmful when starting a new job. They're stumbling over being able to communicate, connect and build relationships with others.

How do friends and family affect our lives?

In many cases, immediate family can think it's okay to contact you at any time, so it's important to set boundaries. If that makes you uncomfortable, then only allow yourself to check your phone messages and personal emails when you're on a break.

However, it's also important to understand that when it comes to one of them needing help, they should be your first priority. Also, acknowledging them for all they do is a great way to let them know you appreciate how they're always there for you.

Remember to give the majority of your time to your loyal friends. Those who've been there for you. There are people who will come into your life that look like shiny diamonds, but when you need to lean on them, they're nowhere to be found. Learn to spot the difference between those who will stand by your side and the ones who will leave you in a time of crisis.

What does success mean to you?

- Getting started.
- Taking three steps forward and only one back.
- Learning the process of new lessons.
- Becoming proficient in what I've learned.
- Getting my first hired helper.
- Knowing I truly helped someone succeed in life.
- Having my confidence elevated.
- Knowing I've helped someone in need.
- Loving the learning process.
- Helping more souls reach their own pinnacle in life and sport.
- Answering a cry for help and assisting in a successful outcome.
- Knowing I'm halfway to my outcome goal.
- Counting the hundreds of gratitude statements I've made over the years.
- Achieving my generational legacy for my children to take over the business.

What's the best success tip you could ever give anyone?

Learn to keep focused long enough to go the distance, never give up and finish strong.

 To discover more about how Ivena can help you *Elevate Your Performance*, simply visit

www.elevatebooks.com/performance

Afterword

While you were reading these people's inspiring stories, did you notice something? All of their life experiences were for a purpose, bringing them closer to their goals, relationships and especially the message they were meant to share with the world.

The last page is a blank canvas for you to write the next chapter of your own story about elevating your performance and inspiring others. Every day is a brand-new opportunity to be the author of your destiny.

Next Steps

To support you on your journey to *Elevate Your Performance,* we recommend you take advantage of these resources:

🖥 7 Day Transformation Program

Learn ONE powerful 'Elevate Process' you can use immediately to improve Your Relationships, Health, Finances, Mindset and any other area of your life.

To join this 7-day transformation online program, simply go to: www.elevatebooks.com/you

👥 Connect with the Authors

To discover more about the authors and what they have to teach you, and bonus gifts they are offering visit:
www.elevatebooks.com/performance

🎤 Subscribe to our Podcast

If you'd like to hear the go-to interviews from the authors and be re-inspired, check out: www.elevatebooks.com/podcast

🌐 Visit the Website

To find out more about the Elevate book series, visit: www.elevatebooks.com

www.ingramcontent.com/pod-product-compliance
Lightning Source LLC
Chambersburg PA
CBHW071602080526
44588CB00010B/991